ON THE CELLAR DOOR
And All that Goes with Winter
by Dave Gregory

EMERALD LAKE
BOOKS

*It has been a tradition in our house
that Santa's helpers set up shop in the cellar.*

*Every year around Thanksgiving
a notice to that effect
shows up on the cellar door ...*

This book is dedicated to the small body of family and friends who inspire, encourage and tolerate my writing.

Introduction

On the Cellar Door has very humble origins. It grew as my children grew. Once my kids could read, a sign would go up on the cellar door around Thanksgiving time. The original signs were simple orders, "KEEP OUT." Somewhere along the line, I started to expand on this theme and would write a little poem, ending with a dire warning for any unauthorized persons who thought to cross the threshold.

The cellar was the main storage and assembly point for our family's Christmas presents. Originally, we waited until Christmas Eve to put up the tree, assemble and wrap the presents and put out the milk and cookies. Actually, in our house it was beer and cookies, after all Santa needed some reward from his helpers.

This Christmas Eve assembly/ decorating lunacy lasted a year or two and died in the face of a dollhouse that required one hundred thirty-six screws and nuts to construct.

Still... The buying, wrapping and giving are a constant joy, year after year, even though I don't do much assembly these days.

In one of those moments that parents hate, the maturing children let slip, revealed, bragged or "snitched" that the signs had generally been ignored and that some Christmas morning surprises were actually Academy Award-winning performances.

The first *On the Cellar Door* poem I saved was from 1992. The next year the poem was titled *Dave's Christmas Poem – 1993*. Stirs the imagination doesn't it? The first poem for public consumption came in 1994 and was copied onto red or green paper and included in a few Christmas cards to family and friends.

Sometime during 1995, my wife and I took bridge lessons. It was there we met Beth Williams and her husband, Russ. We started to practice playing cards outside of class and a friendship resulted. Beth has decorated my *On the Cellar Door* poems from 1995 to the present day. Her whimsy has helped my words look better and she continually challenges herself to be original.

The second part of this book, *And All that Goes with Winter*, includes stories and poems that help portray my love/hate relationship with the winter season. In this section, you'll be reminded of joyous preparations and fond memories of the Christmas season, and the short days and long nights of cold that follow until spring finally makes it a thing of the past.

Artwork for these pages is provided by M. (Maggie) Macy. I met Maggie in September 1962 during Orientation Week at Boston University. We were both incoming freshman and became friends almost instantly. During the early '70s, we lost track of each other and life went on.

A couple of years back, I was sharing stories with my kids and mentioned this talented artist and poet I once knew and of those days back in Boston and some years after. My son hit the computer and found Maggie up in Maine. I wrote to confirm and our friendship has picked up where it left off.

It turns out we both took that thirty-year break to marry and raise children. Despite the demands of home and family, she continued pursuing her art and her paintings have been exhibited nationwide.

On the Cellar Door

Keep Out!
...because it's almost...
Christmas...

On the Cellar Door – 1992

The leaves have let go and given up,
their gentle rustling
now a plaything on the ground for
kicking and shuffling.
The sun, no longer a star, has begun
a supporting role,
to warm the heart with memories,
but not the body.
The wind has taken center stage.
Mariah now controls.
Bringing clippers and fronts and
pushing the calendar to its end.
Ridding the trees of summer survivors
and leaving only spider-webbed
branches to bang the sky with
ugly dances.
But take heart! Hidden among
those faster-moving clouds a
spirit has begun to grow –
One of joy and forgiving –
One of spirit and living –
Spirited in the dark by
gaily-colored elves with
chubby cheeks and great-looking hats.
They've taken residence in
cellars and attics and in the
back of closets all over the world.
They work and wait for their boss to come.
They're shy...
SO KEEP THE HELL AWAY –
AND MERRY CHRISTMAS!

Dave's Christmas Poem – 1993

The empty branches are wrestling with the wind.
Leaves have surrendered to the first line of cold –
No longer fragile shade for our world,
but rather crinkling pleasure for our kicking,
piled high for jumping,
a faint memory of their burning fragrance.

A sky full of late afternoon color,
as rich as the leaves of a month ago –
Clouds threatening,
no longer drifting,
but moving now with purpose.

The shortened daylight has people rushing
to find the indoors.
The hours' length seems
somehow bitten by a frost
that will only thaw
when spring's sunrise comes
some months from now.

We have treated and thanked.
Now what's left is celebration –
The birth of a God-child, a new year,
a miracle of lights –
A time of giving.

A single candle through a frozen night
"flames" the Word.
It is time again to sing!
Carols of praise, telling of stories,
decorations of happiness, wreathes of love –
Light of renewal.

Children's time at any age
for first wonder of the red-suited giver.
The laughter of the world turned into
their "very most perfect" dream.

And with all this,
you must do your part.
It is as simple as waking
and as hard as watching
the clock climb its hours.
You must stay away – keep from –
not trespass into or climb down to –
That which is below,
because if you enter that world,
webs longer than a spider's spinning lifetime
will wrap you to the fire of "Scroogedom."

All fears will become real.
Only socks and underwear
will greet your gaze.
Surprises will collapse in the tears of
"Batteries not included."
You will have to assemble it yourself
and the directions will be in a language
you've never seen before.
It will all be something you already
have or never wanted.

So the door will stay closed and
will open on Christmas Morning with
all the love we can manage.

We love you and will kick you if you peek.

On the Cellar Door – 1994

The color that filled the trees a while ago
has drained into mid-afternoon sunsets.
What used to hold red, yellow and orange
has fallen into kick'n crunchy brown.
Those gentle breezes that brought us relief
now chill our shoulders and numb our feet.
Lazy days of relaxing have turned to
tense hustling to get home before dark.
Pumpkins and pilgrims have paid their brief visit
and we are left facing the cellar door.

What's behind the cellar door?
Ferlinghetti's pink plastic tree,
a three-sided balsam with needles
falling before it's mounted,
color-coded branches
with instructions from a foreign land?
Or the most beautiful tree,
balanced and secure and decorated to your taste?

Behind the door?
Is it the spirit of the wise men carrying the world?
No, it can't be. That's absurd!
Is it the faith that God's son has come and gone
and may come again in our hearts?
Is it the spirit of red and green and cherubic song
from the most ungainly voices?

The gifts given, spilling from room to room,
or just as lovingly
barely covering the edge of the tattered skirt –
It doesn't matter.

My train set, my soldier set,
My model '56 Corvette,
Santa's footprints.
Your blonde doll, your sweaters,
your clothes, your Nerf football, bubble stuff –
Rumbling in the heart.

Behind the cellar door are this year's gifts
and those to come and those all done.
It is Christmas –
And to cross the threshold
and diminish the surprise –
Well, it's unkind to the givers
and, frankly,
could result in pain to the trespasser,
for we all know that
"He who peeks turns into a balloon!"

On the Cellar Door – 1995

The clouds are puffing across the sky,
like a toy locomotive rounding the Christmas tree.
As I set my rake aside
the wind whips a new supply of leaves from hiding.

The maples have let go their color.
The oak has given the squirrel his autumn labor.
The sun gives off a faint warming,
pushed aside easily by the lengthening night.

The Season has begun
with store displays competing with Columbus
and the havens of collectibles
that take the name the whole year 'round.

And for who is this red and green season?
Those wide-eyed, cherub-cheeked believers?
The ones with visions and no inhibitions
and winter coats buttoned tight below their chins?

The little ones who love the Jesus baby
and sit on Father's shoulders to see
Santa on a fire truck for picture-taking
and giving lists of things long wished for.

Who are these Bert and Ernie believers
barely able to walk and talk?
And how are they so full of
myths and wonder and awe?

Where did they hear these stories
of wise men and kings –
Frosty, Rudolph, Scrooge,
and jolly old St. Nick?

What gave them the faith
to stand up to the cold
with joy and wonder
in things they just understand?

Stand before this door
and see it as a mirror.
Don't hide behind eggnog and years.
It's you who are the believer.

You were they and now spread the word.
You believe in what you heard
because you saw that gentle smile
and knew that all this was true.

So look at the door for what it is –
A gateway to the season.
And don't look beyond it
for any reason.

'Cause if you do
you'll catch the bottom of my shoe,
and coal and cold will be
what's left behind on that December morning.

Goodwill and happiness
to last and last and last
till it's time for a new bunch of believers.
Maybe yours.

On the Cellar Door – 1996

Christmas is built in layers.
Childhood memories and family traditions,
religion and commercialism
blending with maturity.

The greatest story ever told
mixes with the greatest toy ever wanted.
The giggling caroler is suddenly singing loudly,
warmed by the hot cider
and the tears in the old woman's eyes.

The race begun in the season of many colors
is finally won on the red and green morning
of squealing delight.

We have lonely times
when we have "lost" or grown "too old"
before we find the spirit and succumb.

The winter songs are never played
after December,
so we must cram the season in.

The selection or resurrection
of the tree, balsam or blue spruce,
real or artificial.

Crisp mornings
with tattered brown leaves
frozen in last night's frost.
The beauty of that first sheet of white
on a bed of green.

Sounds of talking reindeer
mixed with Santa's promises
lead to restless anticipation
and the formal Polaroid.

Decorations just so or
"Can you believe that?"
"Buy this" or "It's just right."
We've finally got it done.

Winter's right description,
the music – it's all around –
singing softly in awe of His coming
or loudly in celebration.

And the memories of childhood pals –
Frosty friends, choruses of chipmunks,
choirs and stars all talk around
God's creation.

Country or city,
bitter cold or sand,
the candles burn
as we hang our ornaments of life
on that perfect place.
The imperfect is turned to the wall,
at least for now.

The cocoa is hot with marshmallows floating,
real, mini or fluff.
As with most things about Christmas,
there's never enough.

What lies below are the fruits of Christmas,
harvested mostly with love, care and thought,
with only a touch of obligation.
Like most fruit, out of season, it must ripen.

To disturb this process could cause serious damage.
Tags could fall off, tape could loosen,
and grumpy old people
could find their register receipts.

Behind the Cellar Door – 1997

It stands in the corner – It stands by the wall.
It stands on a table – It stands on the floor.
It comes from a forest – It comes from a farm.
It comes from the attic – It comes from a store.
It's plastic or metal – It's balsam or fir.
It stands in a stand – It stands in a ball.
It's a decoration or symbol
standing proud in a skirt.

It can go up days before or on that special eve.
It can stay for a day or stay for a week.
It can stay the rest of the year or more.
It can be hugged by strings of popcorn.
It can be wrapped in gold or silver garland.
It can be warmed by mini or old-fashioned.
It may have bubbles, blinkers, chasers or more.
It now stands ready for the ornamentation.

Bows and baubles of all one color, a lovely confection.
A hodgepodge, an everything collection.
Now it's a memory, a true family tree.

Tinsel and Bells – Tinsel and Bells
Cardinals and snowflakes,
butterflies and plastic-faced elves –
That was what we could afford.
Tinsel and Bells – Tinsel and Bells
Apples and candy canes,
a fragile ornament
from a tree of your past.
Tinsel and Bells – Tinsel and Bells
Gone are the
silver icicles and
spray cans of snow.
Tinsel and Bells – Tinsel and Bells
The golden sister star,
Grandmothers' and kids' loving constructions.
"Fill in that hole over there."
Tinsel and Bells – Tinsel and Bells
All this with the children's annual selections
and our lifetime acquisitions.
Tinsel and Bells – Tinsel and Bells
Finally, the tree topper.
Baby-faced angel – Stained glass star
"Get it straight" – "Now"
Look down on all the Tinsel and Bells.

What will flow from under the tree?
Who can tell? No, don't tell!
That's the naughty and nice thing
all over again.
It's between Santa and his elves
what might be behind this door.
But one elf knows, if you go and peek,
he'll hold his breath till you turn purple.

On the Cellar Door – 1998

The King swaddled in a manger,
wise men and shepherds in attendance.
The night filled with song,
guided by a single light.
This is what it's about.

Autumn winds chasing summer breezes
into winter gales.
Crisp moonlight outlining clouds
against the night sky.
This is what it's about.

People guided to the mall
by stars and celebrities,
clamoring for the latest
of what's not available.
This is what it's about?

All the stories and tales,
the miracles and the magic –
Santa Claus, Rudolph and Frosty,
Littlest Tree, O Tannenbaum, fa la.
This is what it's about.

Snow-covered fields,
trees trimmed and standing tall.
Sleds and skis and saucers
crashing down the hill.
This is what it's about.

Sunday morning sunshine –
Folks filing through the vestry,
some for the first time since Easter,
filling His House to hear the story.
This is what it's about?

Children wishing, people rushing,
spirits rising to the day.
New and old traditions –
Families warmed by being together.
This is what it's about.

Behind the door, ribbon and wrapping
and great confusion.
Elders and elves working
to a point of delusion.
This is what it's about.

Crossing the threshold
and being a lowly age
can cause dust and rot
and dreaded parental rage.

Behind the Cellar Door — 1999

Night creeping into sunrise —
Water going blue to gray —
We've passed the mud and bulb season —
The "wiggle" toes in grass season —
The kick the leaves and pumpkin season —
To the most festive of them all!

Our prescriptions for the year
have just about run out.
The colors fold from rust
to red and green and haloed yellow.
The slow pace of warmer weather
is pushed into higher gear.

We can see the snow-covered fields
of our dreams and expectations
lying fresh and waiting for
new footsteps to mark the trail
or little wool-bound creatures ready
to flop and make angels real.

It is fast becoming the time
to take small hands, wrinkled hands
and empty hands into ours,
telling the small hands stories
of that special night and
all the others built around it.

Time to thank the wrinkled hands
for teaching you the same stories
when your hands were small,
taking hold of the empty hands
and holding them extra tight
letting them know it's all right.

Memories tumble inside our heads
and fall in smiles and tears.
Take the happier ones —
Let them come shining through.
We can stand up and turn around,
tap our toes on the frozen ground.

Do you see? Do you see?
The man running down Main Street –
Wishing "Merry Christmas!"
to everything in sight.
And whiskered jolly winking
bowl-full of "yelly", nods of delight.

Trees, trees and more trees
inside and out –
Full of bubble lights
and blinking lights –
Holding memories, not quite straight,
glass and plastic ornaments
different – All the same.

Songs crashing the heights –
Choirs and cowboys.
Oh, he's gone this year –
"Like a lightbulb."
We'll have to sing for him,
louder and without fear.

Finding the gift to give us a lift
to keep the young ones "oh-wowing,"
the older ones nodding with delight.
It was the right size! Out of sight!
And not to be a "Grumpy Stiltskin."
Receive it! It's given to you. Same love.

Can all this come to one night
and dawn a wonderful morning?
Hold us warm for the rest of the winter
with snowflakes falling. Taste the cold.
Puddles vanishing beneath the ice –
Evergreens sagging to the ground.

It can. We can. It does.
For it is a season of everything right –
Love and beliefs, giving and singing
anticipation and resolutions
complaining and spending and
loving and laughing and you.

From the North Pole, comes the final word
"I've got these helpers working late.
They want your day to be special.
Behind this door, they've put in storage
great ideas or if you look
only gruel and porridge!"

On the Cellar Door – 2000

The trees have shed their autumn color.
The ocean is on its way from blue to gray.
Formations crowd the sky.
The growing has been upended.

Christmas comes before the clouds of winter,
before we know it the days are short.
Christmas comes before the darkness.
It is a foundation for a little hope.

Can you see? Can you see?

The farmhouse beside the snowy fields
nestled in the shadow of the green-black forest.
Family by the fireplace, stringing popcorn
for an old-fashioned tree. Child on father's knee.
Stories of the season – Memories and recollections.
Tree from their land, decorated simply,
fastened with values and understanding.
Topped by an angel – Topped by a star.

Can you see? Can you see?

The small town's street ablaze with color,
neighbor trying to outdo neighbor.
More icicles. More reindeer.
More corny, wonderful decorations.
The house down the street – Right there –
Adding to their memories, laughing.
Real snowman. Real feelings.
Topped by an angel – Topped by a star.

Can you see? Can you see?

The busy city's cluster, look inside.
Hidden among the steel and apathy,
little lights of loneliness
and others warming to the grand occasion.

Family gathered by the artificial tree
talking of where they're from,
their history from real canyons to these.
Topped by an angel – Topped by a star.

Can you see? Can you see?
Starlight, filling the night,
bringing out our dreams, our hopes.
Our imagination in sight.

The guiding star gleaming on a winter night,
leading wise men, shepherds and their flock.
Stars used by explorers and lost souls
to reach newfound destinations.

Stars to top the trees and
carry the angels' chorus to our hearts.
To find our star and let it lead us –
A lifetime quest. We can only do our best.

I have my star. It has me in its grasp.
The day must only pass, and it is there again.
It glimmers and shines. Why, yes, it twinkles!
Or it is clouded by the moves of God and nature.

It looks so small and sometimes far away.
Other times, so close you can touch it.
In the universe of speed and bustle,
it is my oasis, feet planted on the ground.

The festive glow of cherry cheeks,
of growing and longing and loving.
We wish upon our chosen star
and hope to share the road of light.

I have my star. Your star?
Can you see? Can you see?

The starlight, leading to this cellar
is fraught with danger for early peekers.
It's not a case of woolen mittens or
nice multicolored and variegated sneakers.
It is patience for the Christmas morn,
with music, the tree, the lights, the "ooga" horn.

On the Cellar Door – 2001

What if the color of Christmas were gone?
No red or green, no festive celebration.
Gone the delight on the children's faces.
Gone the songs from the sanctuary.

What if winter passed in total neglect?
No Before and After sales. No rushing.
Gone the trees and preparation.
Gone the stories and the fables.

What if the world stood empty?
No tasteful, tacky, blinking decorations.
Gone the cards and presents.
Gone the meaning and spirit.

What if we forget what it was about?
No birthday-manger recollection.
Gone the depression and happiness.
Gone the wonder. Gone the wonder.

Only a small part of each person
believes in what-ifs.
Friends, faith and family
bring everything to life.

Holding a friend's gaze for a moment –
A simple smile can warm the heart.
And the "I love you"
can make it soar.

So pull out, cut down, straighten up
your blue spruce or balsam.
Ring the bells. Start the choirs.
Make way for red-nosed flyers.

Forget about the summer.
Cover up the fall.
Lay down a blanket of white
and wait for that special night.

Ride the cold wind
from store to store.
Find a gift worth giving.
Meanings, do not ignore.

Run from here to there.
Hang up – Shake out –
Kindle the fire and the memories.
Remember the wonder, that wonder.

Now behind this door,
you'll find Christmas in the making.
Stuff ready for baking.
But cross the threshold too soon –

And cookies will crumble,
the cakes won't rise.
You'll see the disappointment
in your parents' eyes.

ON THE CELLAR DOOR

On the Cellar Door – 2001

What if the color of Christmas were gone?
No red or green, no festive celebration.
Gone the delight on the children's faces.
Gone the songs from the sanctuary.

What if winter passed in total neglect?
No Before and After sales. No rushing.
Gone the trees and preparation.
Gone the stories and the fables.

What if the world stood empty?
No tasteful, tacky, blinking decorations.
Gone the cards and presents.
Gone the meaning and spirit.

What if we forget what it was about?
No birthday-manger recollection.
Gone the depression and happiness.
Gone the wonder. Gone the wonder.

Only a small part of each person
believes in what-ifs.
Friends, faith and family
bring everything to life.

Holding a friend's gaze for a moment –
A simple smile can warm the heart.
And the "I love you"
can make it soar.

So pull out, cut down, straighten up
your blue spruce or balsam.
Ring the bells. Start the choirs.
Make way for red-nosed flyers.

Forget about the summer.
Cover up the fall.
Lay down a blanket of white
and wait for that special night.

Ride the cold wind
from store to store.
Find a gift worth giving.
Meanings, do not ignore.

Run from here to there.
Hang up – Shake out –
Kindle the fire and the memories.
Remember the wonder, that wonder.

Now behind this door,
you'll find Christmas in the making.
Stuff ready for baking.
But cross the threshold too soon –

And cookies will crumble,
the cakes won't rise.
You'll see the disappointment
in your parents' eyes.

IN THE CELLAR DOOR

On the Cellar Door – 2002

"Yeah! It's morning!"
Parents take warning,
I've been as good as I could
for as long as I could.
"Come on. Come on! Get up. Get up!
We gotta go downstairs
and see if Santa's come.
Mom, Dad... Come on!"
To the top of the stairs
and then starting down,
peeking through the banister.
"Yes! Presents! He's been here.
Oh, the tree. The lights!"
Running to the foot of the tree,
then frozen, eyes searching
the presents piled in careful confusion.
"What's for me? What's for me?"
Foil and paper, ribbon and bows,
tissue and tape, bags and boxes,
sharp corners, just so
extra folds, extra paper, extra tape.
Red and green, blue and stripes,
snowmen, hymn notes, solids and patterns,
Santas old and new,
snow scenes, skaters and reindeered sleighs,
all hiding what's good from sight.
Toys and things needed and toys.
Toys and (ugh!) clothes and toys.
Things asked for, things a surprise.
"I made this for you, Mom."
"Dad, I made a picture for your work."
Toys and toys and... Wow! Toys!
Finally a package way under the tree,
wrapped neatly in angel paper.
A gift, a family gift,
not just for me.
The gift of the meaning of Christmas,
sometimes lost in the scraps.
The gift of a son,
of love and of hope,
of understanding, of peace.
It's for me. It's for you.
Now that the preparation has begun
and things are beginning to be done,
move away from the door.
Don't spoil what's in store
because if you start peeking,
your nose I'll be tweaking.

PART I

ON THE CELLAR DOOR

Come take a walk,
midway through December.
It's a week till winter
and a few more days
till the celebration.

Bundle them up, line them up.
Check scarves and mittens,
hats tied under chins,
boots and socks and wooly, wooly layers —
"Ready? Come on..."

It's a crisp night
with the wind pushing and pulling.
The moon and stars racing with
some puffy white clouds.
Our breath is haloed in the streetlight.

We stroll on a thin layer
of hard-packed snow
that has caught some brown leaves and
kept them from further flight.
Feet crunching in the quiet night.

Now, let's go down the street.
First one side and
back up the other.
Look at every window.
Check out all the doors.

The white palace with white spotlights
lighting the white house,
with a tree of white lights
in the big front window —
A wreath with white bow on the door.

Then pass by the houses of variations —
Green mini lights, red mini lights,
blue mini lights,
white mini lights, multicolor mini lights —
Netted or strung on bushes and trees.
Icicle lights strung from the gutters.
Big lights outlining its frame.

At least one Clark Griswold
whose yard reflects
all the Season's favorite tales.
Plastic Frostys, Nutcracker soldiers,
Rudolphs and more.
White deer nod and graze at the back,
and God's only son is huddled
close to the juniper.

Lights chase and blink and glow,
row after row after row after row.
Santa waves from atop his chimney
and all seems quieter as we move on by.

We could sing a carol or two,
something simple,
something for everyone tonight.
What if we wander on
and tell Christmas stories,
or think back to when
Aunt So-and-So gave us —
Or you had the best time when...

Maybe we'll think of cider or hot cocoa
or eggnog at walk's end.
Maybe we'll think of the reason
for the decorations.

And passing the last house, almost dark,
with just a silly little group of bells,
some patched-up greens
hanging on the door.
The same as last year.
The same as all the years.
And we'll smile and be filled
with memories.

"Race you home."
"And close the door!"
We had a moment 'round the embers
of our hearts.

Now the time has come for warning.
Beyond this door,
you're not free to explore
while Mom and Dad snore.
But if your feet start down these steps,
bubblegum will stick to your hair,
licorice will pop out of your ears —
You may dream of what's in store,
and you'll cry chicken parmesan tears.

On the Cellar Door – 2004

In the land of Ribbons and Bows,
you get what you want.
In the village of Gotta Have Things,
In the neighborhood of We're Better Than You,
In the house of See What We Got,
Lives the family of We Have to Have More.

They work hard every day, no doubt about it.
They make plenty of loot and commission.
Some say they deserve what they get.
Others are jealous and question their mission.

'Round the bend, over the hill,
or on the other side of those famous tracks,
the other fraction of faction lives.
Working just as hard and some longer hours,
raising a family with the same love and intuition.

Now that the calendar has changed
and you have to wear socks –
Now that the leaves have colored
and run away with the sun –
It's time to shop!

So both these groups, known one to the other,
start thumbing the catalogues,
running to the store and mall places,
in search of what's right and needed,
or in fashion or perfect or "awww!"

The noise and commotion
blurs lines and distinctions.
What rises above and is set in motion
is the love of giving, the good wishes,
the good feeling eruption.

And when one steps back,
you see what's in common.
On a Friday night or Sunday morning,
a celebration of light, the oil burning for days,
or the celebration of a birth
guided by a single star's light.

Can there be a better time to raise voices to heaven?
Thank God for the gifts that He's given?
To come close to our family and friends?
To talk to Santa and reindeer
and bright golden rings?
To remember all good things, no matter how sad?

To imagine that star's light
or light a candle every night?
To smile at the wee ones' delight
and remember all our good nights?

The warning. The warning! Watch out. Watch out!
Boxes and things yet unmade
lie at the foot of the stairs.
Maybe it's toys.
Maybe it's some Barbie dishes.
Nevertheless, you must wait
and store up your wishes
'cause if you peek or take a look…
Why, why, why… I'm gonna cry!

On the Cellar Door – 2004

In the land of Ribbons and Bows,
you get what you want.
In the village of Gotta Have Things,
In the neighborhood of We're Better Than You,
In the house of See What We Got,
Lives the family of We Have to Have More.

They work hard every day, no doubt about it.
They make plenty of loot and commission.
Some say they deserve what they get.
Others are jealous and question their mission.

'Round the bend, over the hill,
or on the other side of those famous tracks,
the other fraction of faction lives.
Working just as hard and some longer hours,
raising a family with the same love and intuition.

Now that the calendar has changed
and you have to wear socks –
Now that the leaves have colored
and run away with the sun –
It's time to shop!

So both these groups, known one to the other,
start thumbing the catalogues,
running to the store and mall places,
in search of what's right and needed,
or in fashion or perfect or "awww!"

The noise and commotion
blurs lines and distinctions.
What rises above and is set in motion
is the love of giving, the good wishes,
the good feeling eruption.

And when one steps back,
you see what's in common.
On a Friday night or Sunday morning,
a celebration of light, the oil burning for days,
or the celebration of a birth
guided by a single star's light.

Can there be a better time to raise voices to heaven?
Thank God for the gifts that He's given?
To come close to our family and friends?
To talk to Santa and reindeer
and bright golden rings?
To remember all good things, no matter how sad?

To imagine that star's light
or light a candle every night?
To smile at the wee ones' delight
and remember all our good nights?

The warning. The warning! Watch out. Watch out!
Boxes and things yet unmade
lie at the foot of the stairs.
Maybe it's toys.
Maybe it's some Barbie dishes.
Nevertheless, you must wait
and store up your wishes
'cause if you peek or take a look…
Why, why, why… I'm gonna cry!

On the Cellar Door – 2005

Dear Santa,

I want – I want – I want – I want –
Toys – Toys – Toys – Toys –
Well clothes too, all sorts of things.
The same stuff my friends have,
but better, bigger, brighter. For me!
I want the prettiest tree.
I want snow on Christmas Eve.
I want decorations, better than next door.
I want everything. I deserve it.
I want – I want – I want – I want –
You to be happy too.
I guess I'll share some of what I get.
I mean you can have some stuff too.
It's okay. Want some of my presents?
I mean, I'll loan you some.
Oh! I made this for you. Take it.
Here Mom, Dad – I saved.
Hope you like it.
What? Oh, that's okay. I love it.
Listen. Listen!
Do you hear the carolers?
Bethlehem, kings, shepherds,
angels, stars, wonder, a baby,
a new King, gifts, love.
I want – I want – I want – I want –
All sorts of peace and happiness
for my family and friends.
I want – I want – I want – I want –
An evening sky, bright enough
to guide us.

I want a fire to warm us.
I want smiles from the heart.
I want everyone to be selfish.
I want them to steal thoughts.
I want them to go back.
I want them to go forward.
I want them to remember their
happiest holiday memory.
I want them to use that
as a foundation.
I want them to build
on that foundation
to bring a happy future
without darkening the past.
I want them to continue to grow.
I want them to love
the simplest thing: each other.

I want – I want – I want – I want –
You to stay out of the cellar
'cause if I see footprints in the dust
or hear creaking louder than my knees –
Well, I bet you a bowl of fruit
And a big "patuee"★ there will
be something less for you and your
Brother Louie.

★*Alternate spelling: P-toohey, Ptooey,
Phatooie, Pitoohey, Pahtuy, Patouwi,
Patooie, Puttie, Patuie, Patowe, Petui,
Patwoe, Patooey, Patuey, Petuey or Petuie.*

On the Cellar Door – 2006

Have you seen their eyes?
Noses pressed to glass,
fog spreading across the window,
checking the winter scene.

"When will school ever end?"
The preparations have begun.
The boxes are down.
Serious questions are being asked.

"And what do you
want for Christmas?"
"Ah, ah… I don't know."
"Ho, Ho, Ho!
How about a truck?" Smile!
"Um… That thing on TV.
You know…"

"Can I help set them up?
I'm trying, but they're tangled.
This one doesn't light.
I did check it.
Never mind…
Can I go out and play?"

"What do ya wanna do?"
"I don't know. Whadda you
wanna do?"
"Let's build a snowman,
a fort and a monster."

"Will you take me to the store?
How much does that cost?
Is this enough money?
If I like it, Mom will too…"

"Do I have to go?
But my shoes hurt.
Yes, I brushed them.
Yes, I'm coming. Hey! Wait for me!"

"Can we sit in the balcony?
I know this story,
I know this song,
Sle–ep in hea–ven–ly pea–ce."

"What do the shepherds hear?
The kings bring gold,
frankincense and myrrh.
What's myrrh?
Hey! That's not a real baby!
But… LET US ADORE HIM…"

"How long are we gonna be?
Hi Gramps, Hi Granma.
Yeah… I wear it all the time.
Can I go play in back?"

"Is that one going to be ours?
It's almost straight.
Can I hang this one on?
When are we going to… Aahhh!"

"Can I stay up a little longer?
Yes, the milk and cookies
are out.
That's not fair.
Why should I?
But I'm not sleepy."

Have you seen their eyes
trying to peek down cellar?
Checking closets,
helping with bundles.
Watch it! If you're caught,
it's icicles on your nose
and petunias
between your toes.

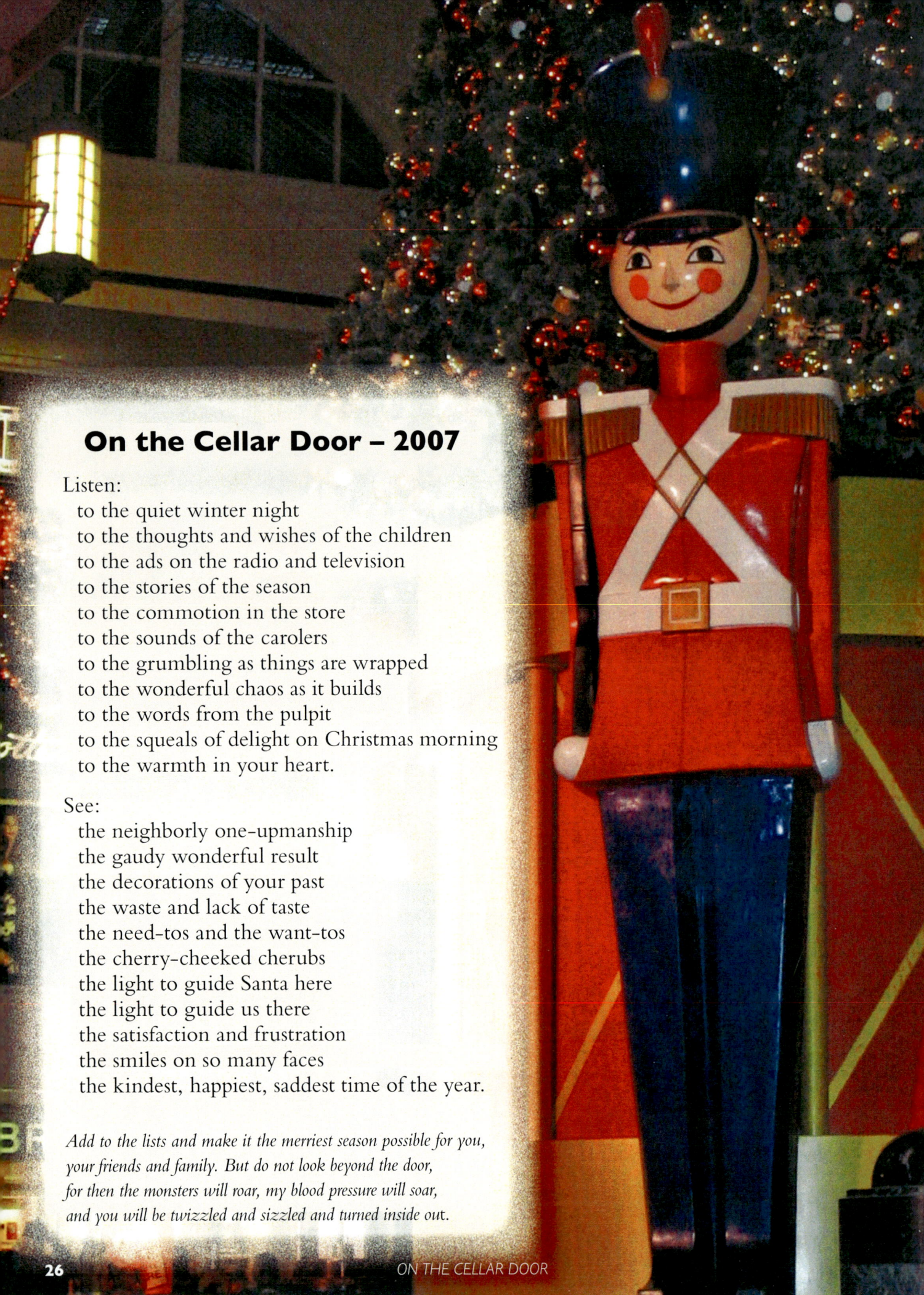

On the Cellar Door – 2007

Listen:
    to the quiet winter night
    to the thoughts and wishes of the children
    to the ads on the radio and television
    to the stories of the season
    to the commotion in the store
    to the sounds of the carolers
    to the grumbling as things are wrapped
    to the wonderful chaos as it builds
    to the words from the pulpit
    to the squeals of delight on Christmas morning
    to the warmth in your heart.

See:
    the neighborly one-upmanship
    the gaudy wonderful result
    the decorations of your past
    the waste and lack of taste
    the need-tos and the want-tos
    the cherry-cheeked cherubs
    the light to guide Santa here
    the light to guide us there
    the satisfaction and frustration
    the smiles on so many faces
    the kindest, happiest, saddest time of the year.

Add to the lists and make it the merriest season possible for you,
your friends and family. But do not look beyond the door,
for then the monsters will roar, my blood pressure will soar,
and you will be twizzled and sizzled and turned inside out.

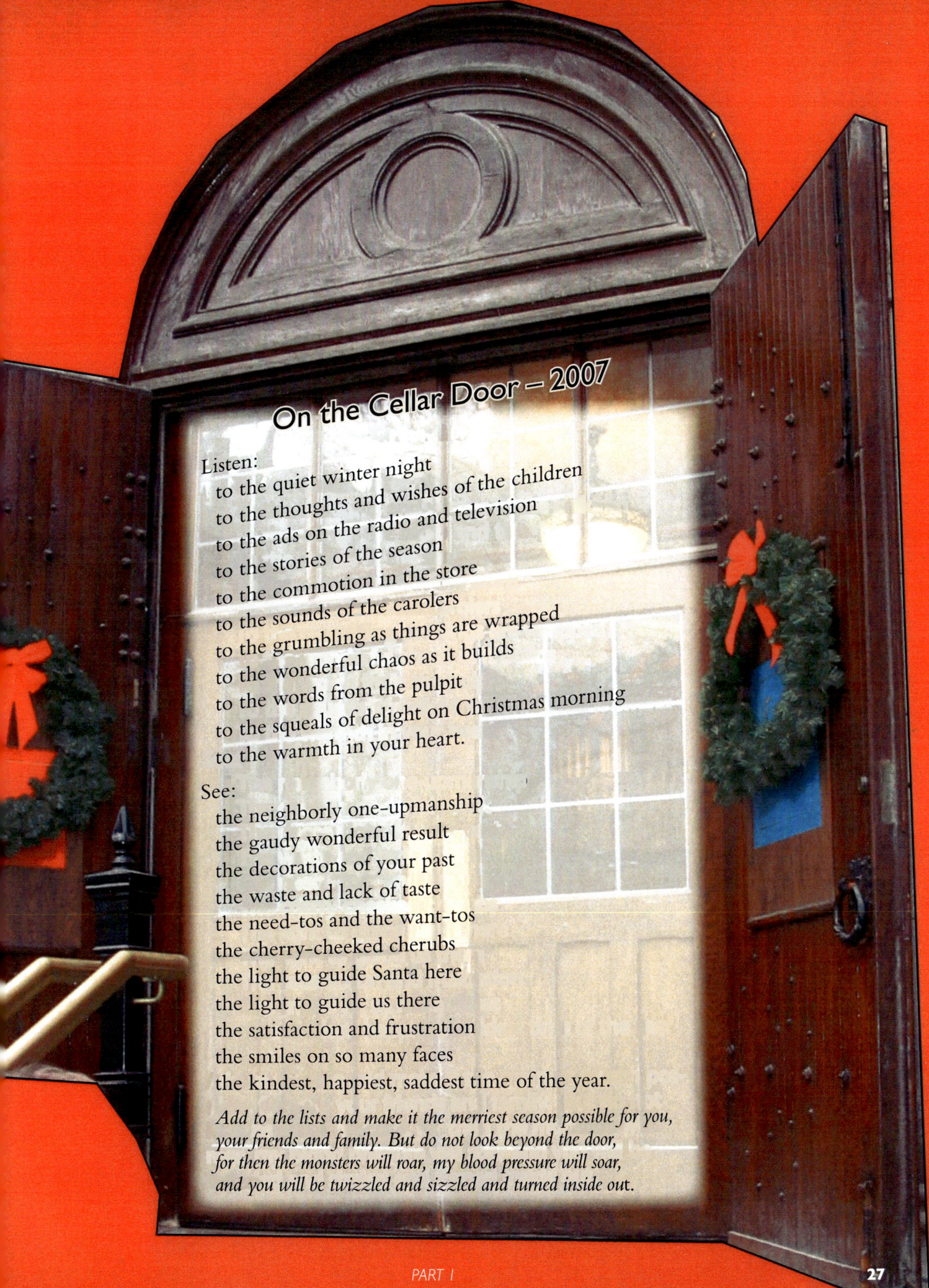

On the Cellar Door – 2007

Listen:
to the quiet winter night
to the thoughts and wishes of the children
to the ads on the radio and television
to the stories of the season
to the commotion in the store
to the sounds of the carolers
to the grumbling as things are wrapped
to the wonderful chaos as it builds
to the words from the pulpit
to the squeals of delight on Christmas morning
to the warmth in your heart.

See:
the neighborly one-upmanship
the gaudy wonderful result
the decorations of your past
the waste and lack of taste
the need-tos and the want-tos
the cherry-cheeked cherubs
the light to guide Santa here
the light to guide us there
the satisfaction and frustration
the smiles on so many faces
the kindest, happiest, saddest time of the year.

Add to the lists and make it the merriest season possible for you,
your friends and family. But do not look beyond the door,
for then the monsters will roar, my blood pressure will soar,
and you will be twizzled and sizzled and turned inside out.

On the Cellar Door – 2008

If I were an…
> I'd want wings to join a heavenly chorus
> and to talk to the people above the clouds.

If I were a…
> I'd want to be crowned with a star or an angel and have,
> hanging below, bright colorful lights and decorations
> from my youth, from my life, from now.

If I were an…
> I'd want a gift, just totally unexpected,
> and I wouldn't grump. Promise.

If I were…
> I'd work to give unselfishly, to spread the word,
> the meaning of it all.

If I were a…
> I'd watch a child's joy, a parent's satisfaction.

If I were a…
> I'd want snow on Christmas Eve,
> and all snowmen and women to be jolly.

If I were…
> I'd celebrate miracles and light the candles each night.

If I were a…
> I'd tell all the stories, all the legends,
> sing all the carols and songs.

If I were…
> I'd try to fill each heart so full
> there would be no room for sadness.

If I were…
> Everything would work. Everything would fit.
> All the batteries would be included. People would be
> with whom they wanted and each song would be sung loudly,
> with trumpets and swelling organs, and with reverence or laughter
> or tears for the memories, happy tears, and all the animals
> would understand.

If I were an…
> Or if I were…
> Everyone would have a joyous holiday.
> A simple wish.

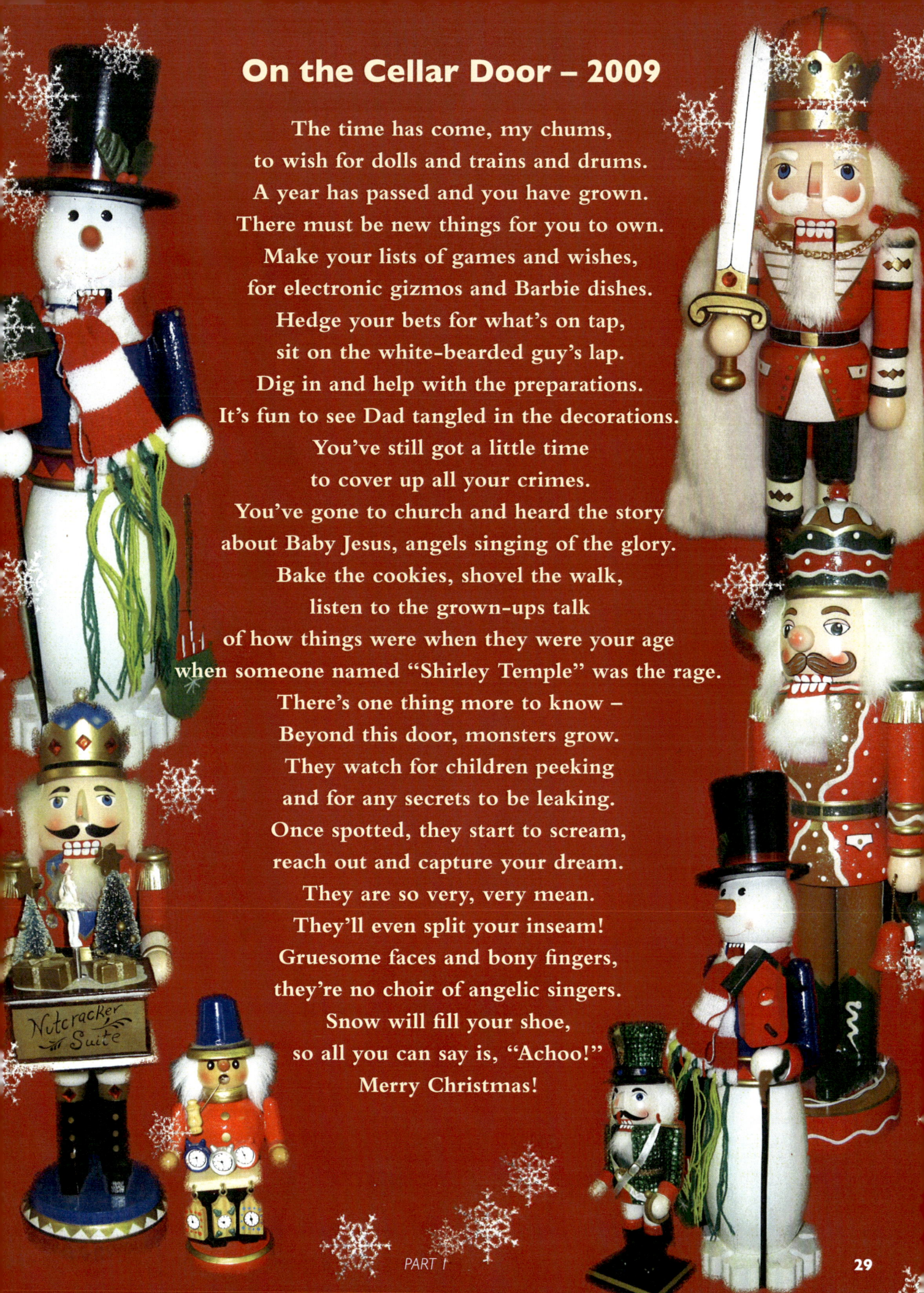

On the Cellar Door – 2009

The time has come, my chums,
to wish for dolls and trains and drums.
A year has passed and you have grown.
There must be new things for you to own.
Make your lists of games and wishes,
for electronic gizmos and Barbie dishes.
Hedge your bets for what's on tap,
sit on the white-bearded guy's lap.
Dig in and help with the preparations.
It's fun to see Dad tangled in the decorations.
You've still got a little time
to cover up all your crimes.
You've gone to church and heard the story
about Baby Jesus, angels singing of the glory.
Bake the cookies, shovel the walk,
listen to the grown-ups talk
of how things were when they were your age
when someone named "Shirley Temple" was the rage.
There's one thing more to know –
Beyond this door, monsters grow.
They watch for children peeking
and for any secrets to be leaking.
Once spotted, they start to scream,
reach out and capture your dream.
They are so very, very mean.
They'll even split your inseam!
Gruesome faces and bony fingers,
they're no choir of angelic singers.
Snow will fill your shoe,
so all you can say is, "Achoo!"
Merry Christmas!

ON THE CELLAR DOOR

On the Cellar Door – 2010

So one ornament says to the other:

"What are we doin' here?"

"Just hanging around."

"No, come on…"

"We're making this pile of pine needles pretty. We're putting smiles on little faces, joy in Mom and Dad's heart, and a tear in Grandpa's eye."

"Yeah, but we're just glass or plastic, construction paper and popsicle sticks."

"We're more than that! We're vacation memories, little kid constructions, firsts and lasts."

"What's on top this year?"

"Not sure… Either an angel heralding Christ's coming or a star leading kings and shepherds to the manger on the night of this birth."

"So, we hang here filling gaps and all these lights snuggle the tree with warmth."

"Hey! Are those kids sneaking toward the cellar door?"

"They'd better not or they'll get nasty noodle noggins, slippery slimy succotash, and grizzly green grapes."

"They've stopped! They're helping; one with Mom in the kitchen, the other with Gramps adding tinsel."

"Dad's down cellar. Listen!"

"Is that any kind of language to use on Christmas Eve?"

On the Cellar Door – 2011

I come falling, twirling, descending
from a gray winter sky.
Silently I glide toward earth
riding the wind's currents.
I have no voice of my own.
My carrier announces my arrival.
Softly I spread myself down,
covering the brown leftovers
of autumn's final moments.
Not satisfied with my arrangement,
the taxi wind moves me
here and there, in piles and drifts.
Then I must survive plow and shovel
till the woolen blobs finally find me.
Now the fun begins with shivering laughter.
I'm bunched and balled and thrown,
hitting and missing targets: friend and foe.
I'm ridden on with sled and sleigh,
crushed in tiny angelic forms.
But most of all I'm constructed –
Forts and ferocious monsters give way
to the traditional homespun construction.
Two... No, better! Three snowballs are rolled.
Stacked large to small, I am ready,
armed with sticks, topped with hat,
scarf about my no-neck junction,
buttons for the Emperor's coat.
Finally eyes, nose and smile
give me my friendly disposition.
I am guardian of these little ones.
I appear and disappear at weather's whim,
but I am always in their heart.
Now should you be at an age of grumbling,
don't spoil the fun by toppling
or go peeking behind cellar doors.
For if you try to spoil the Christmas magic,
I'll melt in your boots and turn your face red.
I'll give up my buttons and
you'll find them in your stockings instead.

On the Cellar Door – 2011

I come falling, twirling, descending
from a gray winter sky.
Silently I glide toward earth
riding the wind's currents.
I have no voice of my own.
My carrier announces my arrival.
Softly I spread myself down,
covering the brown leftovers
of autumn's final moments.
Not satisfied with my arrangement,
the taxi wind moves me
here and there, in piles and drifts.
Then I must survive plow and shovel
till the woolen blobs finally find me.
Now the fun begins with shivering laughter.
I'm bunched and balled and thrown,
hitting and missing targets: friend and foe.
I'm ridden on with sled and sleigh,
crushed in tiny angelic forms.
But most of all I'm constructed –
Forts and ferocious monsters give way
to the traditional homespun construction.
Two... No, better! Three snowballs are rolled.
Stacked large to small, I am ready,
armed with sticks, topped with hat,
scarf about my no-neck junction,
buttons for the Emperor's coat.
Finally eyes, nose and smile
give me my friendly disposition.
I am guardian of these little ones.
I appear and disappear at weather's whim,
but I am always in their heart.
Now should you be at an age of grumbling,
don't spoil the fun by toppling
or go peeking behind cellar doors.
For if you try to spoil the Christmas magic,
I'll melt in your boots and turn your face red.
I'll give up my buttons and
you'll find them in your stockings instead.

On the Cellar Door – 2012

How willingly we give in
to the season, to the spirit.
We crank the scenes into position.
Start the countdown. Here it comes.
Begin the Advent calendar,
open every drawer,
make your list, write the cards,
look for sales, purchase and hide.
Wrapping will come later.
Go to church. You remember where it is.
Decorate, decorate and DECORATE!
Inside and out, lights, bows and tinsel,
old decorations and maybe something new – Ha, ha!
Fill the tabletops and shelves.
Clutter the bushes and make them glow.
Dig out all the traditions.
Remember when you were small?
Wasn't it the best time?
You could wish and wish for this
and be happy if you only got that.
When did you learn to give?
And not just sign off on a gift...
When did the story click in?
Who did you make happy this year?
Now you see this door?
It hides the real world –
That wrapping that still has to be done,
whether the gift comes from Santa
or one of his many elves.
You must not look, not even a peek,
because if you do, pirates may scalp you
and Indians might throw you overboard.
Best you wait till Christmas morning.

On the Cellar Door – 2013

For most, it starts in autumn –
The first chill brings a warning warmth
as we harvest our bounty
and celebrate our Thanksgiving.
We plant the seeds for the next season.
Fields of life are leveled.
All the players come out of hiding.
Lists and wishes are expressed –
Red and green suggestions begin.
They blare out from the television.
Sugared cereal is replaced by new gizmos.
Somewhere a starter's pistol fires
and the race has begun.
Get to the store. Get to the church.
Buy the tie. Buy the story.
Wait! Two stories and all kinds of miracles.
Climb into the attic and load down.
Spread the lights and trimming all around.

Visit the Nutcracker and Santa.
Fill the closets and cellar.
Put up the warning –
Angels and elves are watching
our hopefully unselfish giving.
There may be something for you.
It may need some tender assembly.
Batteries might have to be added
so it can whistle and wink.
Then it must be covered with color
and ribbon and bows and TAPE.
Your job is to stay away.
Behaving and helping couldn't hurt.
But, if you don't, watch out!
Your favorite color won't be there.
Perhaps chewing gum and manatees
Will infest your hair.

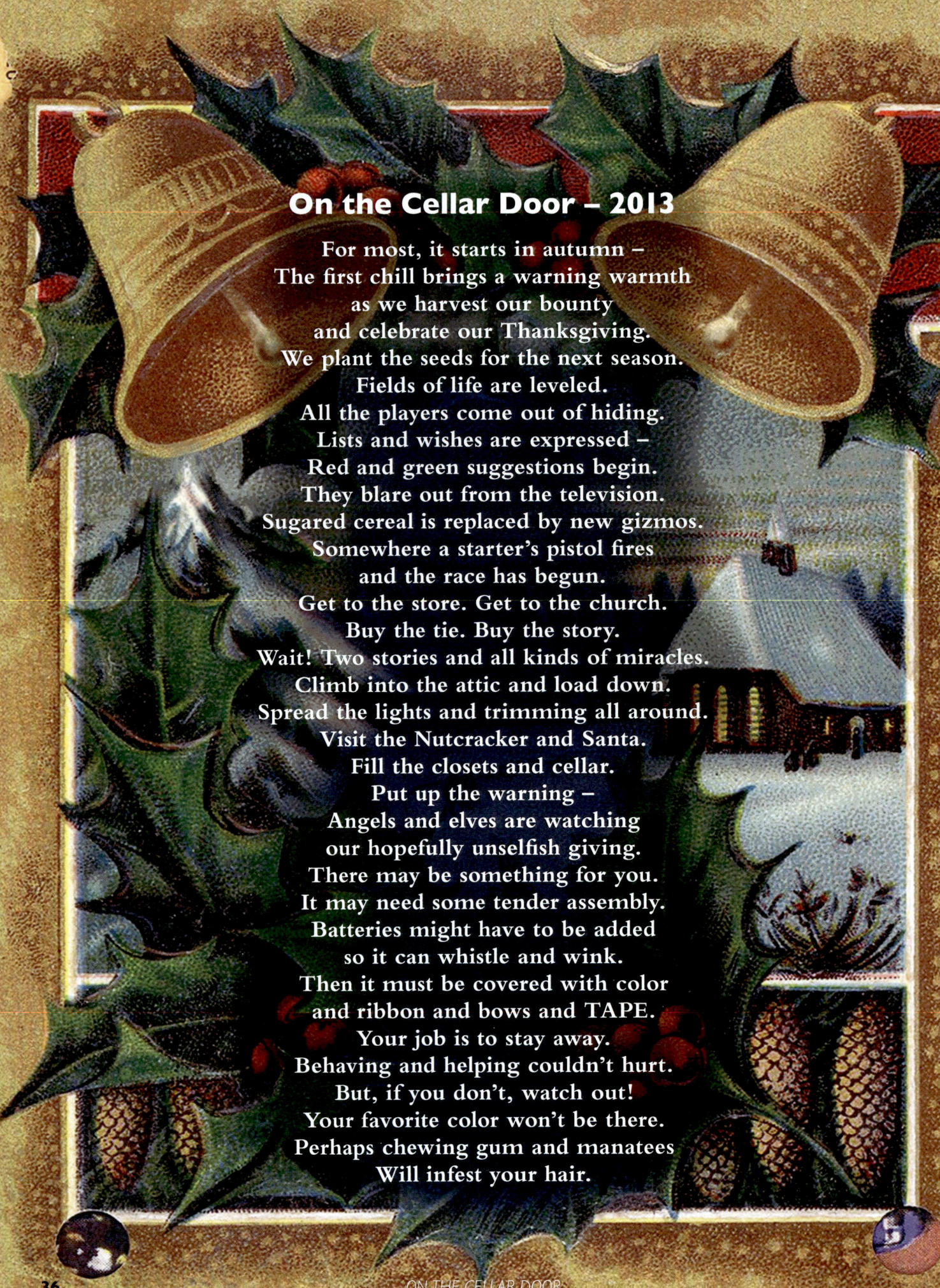

On the Cellar Door – 2013

For most, it starts in autumn –
The first chill brings a warning warmth
as we harvest our bounty
and celebrate our Thanksgiving.
We plant the seeds for the next season.
Fields of life are leveled.
All the players come out of hiding.
Lists and wishes are expressed –
Red and green suggestions begin.
They blare out from the television.
Sugared cereal is replaced by new gizmos.
Somewhere a starter's pistol fires
and the race has begun.
Get to the store. Get to the church.
Buy the tie. Buy the story.
Wait! Two stories and all kinds of miracles.
Climb into the attic and load down.
Spread the lights and trimming all around.
Visit the Nutcracker and Santa.
Fill the closets and cellar.
Put up the warning –
Angels and elves are watching
our hopefully unselfish giving.
There may be something for you.
It may need some tender assembly.
Batteries might have to be added
so it can whistle and wink.
Then it must be covered with color
and ribbon and bows and TAPE.
Your job is to stay away.
Behaving and helping couldn't hurt.
But, if you don't, watch out!
Your favorite color won't be there.
Perhaps chewing gum and manatees
Will infest your hair.

On the Cellar Door – 2014

Ma, look! The Christmas decorations are up!
Never mind... We're late and it's only October.
But, Ma, look! Santa's here!
We'll come back another day. Now come along...
Look! The Griswold's are decorating their yard!
What a waste of money, hmm.
Dad, can I help? I'll be careful.
Thanks, Son, but you better let me take care of it.
What are you going to do this year?
Well, besides the usual, I have a few surprises.
Come on, Dad, tell me. Maybe a manger?
I wove my own deer out of willow branches.
Oh gee, that's swell, Dad. Maybe Mom needs help.
Wait, Son. Watch when I plug it in!
Everybody has deer that nod and graze.
Yeah... But do they have LED lights
and animated pooping?
No, I guess not, Dad. Good job. I'm going in
to watch "Frosty."
Happy Thanksgiving, everybody! Now help
clear the table.
Can we go to church, Mom, please?
Sure, we'll all go. We haven't been in awhile.
I like the story about the Baby Jesus.
I'm glad. Do you know what you're giving your sister?
Yeah, I do. I made it myself.
That's nice, dear. There's a sale at the mall.
Can I come with you? Can we get the tree too?
We'll see. I'll check with your father.
Mom, what's your favorite Christmas carol?
Oh, I don't know. Have you made
your list for Santa?
Yes, Mom, and I helped Sue with hers.
Dear me... Time is flying. I have to
bake cookies.

On the cellar door this magic sign appears.
Keep out, those who are too busy.
Keep out till you're ready to listen.
Don't risk Linguini Lips and Brillo Buns.
Get into the spirit of the season.
Feel the goodness of giving
and the graciousness of receiving.

PART TWO
The Rest of Winter

Winter Begins

And So Winter Begins

The dawn was frightened.
It barely brightened
as rain poxed the ground
and the wind pried free
all that was loose.
It held the curtains closed
and caused us to look away.
The water was swollen
an almost colorless gray
as it lumbered up and down,
mockingly tipping its cap,
rolling with the wind
like some overweight pimp.
The sun finally pushed aside clouds
and the waves settled some.
The wind lessened,
but it was a tease.
Within a couple of hours,
a thick slate tongue
licked the sky somber once more.
The wind changed
and you could hear the cold coming.
The water shifted again,
nervously tipping its cap once more,
but keeping a low profile.
By early afternoon, daylight fades.
There is no white yet,
but its messenger is laying a foundation.
It is finally closing the earth's pores
locking all above ground in place
and holding down new life.
Within a few days, red and green gaiety

will no longer buoy our spirits,
and a week beyond that
the calendar will flop over
leaving us staring at it,
already peeking three pages ahead
and holding our breath till then.
If the next few days or weeks
challenge our emotions –
extreme highs and lows
march heavy-footed through our minds –
Suddenly, unless you are a "snow child,"
you are thrown to the elements
with only the smile of a snowman
to get you through...

December Time

We're just past the natural colors –
Here now the rented ones.
Traditionally we're looking at red and green,
perhaps some blue and gold edging...
Tall monsters holding naked limbs
dance to the wild winds
like rickety veterans of a now-silent ballroom.
Bundles scurry from car to door
or smaller bundles wait for white.
When white comes, construction begins.
Projects beyond Planning and Zoning regulations
appear during the daylight hours.
Forts and tunnels cross property lines
and snowmen add to the current census.
Just done with tucking the garden into bed,
the big ones grow young or harried
as they start to plan and execute.
Some do it as an obligation, another duty to perform –
Others can't wait and steal the mantle of youth –
Gift lists, catalogues and online shopping,
bringing down and opening up
the endless variety of decorations –
Recreating last year or a long ago time,
blending the newest invention
into what works from years past.
Even if it doesn't work anymore,
sometimes it still can fill an empty space,
rest on a shelf lovingly,
or be gently returned to a box
to be discovered next year, with a smile and a tear.

Somewhere along the line we remember
Christmas and Hanukkah.
We find the Menorah and candles.
Church is on the To Do list,
and young and old hear the birthday tale.
Now the young ones hear all the stories.
They are told to be good
because Santa is watching,
and God is always watching.
God and Santa mix in little heads,
but they figure it's time for them to be angels.
They're covering all bets.
Trees, carols, cookies, wrap, hide –
When was the first fruitcake made?
And who gets it this year?
It all builds brightly. It's here.
A brief peak levels and then quickly sinks.
A month or so followed by the worst of winter,
then it's all packed away or discarded.
What's new now blends with the old.
The frozen monotony slowly takes over
and we are left with a fresh layer of memories.

Confessions of a Catalog Junkie

I AM A RECENTLY RETIRED RELUCTANT SENIOR, who enjoys some of the perks of this age, is still surprised to be called "Mr." or "Sir," and is easily flattered to be considered younger.

I am also, according to my mailman, his second best-volume catalog recipient. Whether this is a compliment or a complaint, I'm not sure. He may be just trying to wheedle an extra tube of Bengay for a holiday tip.

The convenience and variety that catalogs present allow me to find gifts that I can match to the people on my list, rather than going into stores and wandering through aisle after aisle and not being happy with the results.

Forgetting the crowds and the hassle, I just pour myself a drink and play an adult version of "Picks," a game my brother and I played in our youth. It started on the first available moment after the arrival of the Sears and Roebuck winter catalog when we were kids. Alternating turns, we went page-by-page "picking" what we wanted for Christmas. The game was usually restricted to the toy or sports equipment sections and was a wish list with no sense of regard for our family's financial status. We didn't expect to get any of these gifts, but loved the game, the dream.

Now let me say that I do indulge in some store shopping. There are certain stores that match my taste in giving and at sometime during the season I visit them.

Wrapping supplies are also usually a better buy in a store. My wrapping-guru daughter insists on a variety of papers under the tree and I must admit that she is right. She also claims that my wife and I started a family tradition of separate Santa paper for stocking gifts. I don't remember this, but happily comply.

I will confess that when it comes to wrapping presents, I am not a bow person. I have had the same three bags of self-adhesive bows for probably ten or twelve years (one unopened and two opened). Every year, if I find them before Christmas, I'll throw on a few.

The heavy catalog season usually runs from about mid-August to mid-November, though there is always a year-round selection to choose from. With this in mind, most of my Christmas is paid for before the holiday or delayed till mid-February depending on what options the different companies offer. The experienced catalog shopper will use the first few catalogs to gather ideas, but wait awhile for the better deals to follow.

Trying not to be an impulse shopper is a constant struggle for me. God, that snow globe that plays fifteen Christmas tunes in all its resin glory would look great in this house! No, I'll wait for the free shipping. I won't have to pay sales tax unless the company is in Connecticut and let us not forget the free personalization.

A fun sideline to catalog shopping is trying to figure how in the hell you got on the mailing list in the first place. This goes hand-in-hand with my pet peeve of how

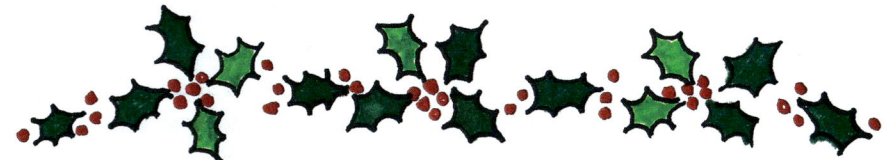

difficult companies make it for the average person to opt out of their sharing your name with other companies. It usually requires an extra call or writing to a separate address and even then they may not honor your request.

An easy way to find out how a company got your name is to vary the spelling of your name, use a middle initial on one application and not on another, etc. We discovered this method quite by accident when Sears sent a credit card with our last name misspelled "Gregor" (having dropped the "y"). They sent a corrected card after their mistake was pointed out to them, but for years "Gregor" lived with us and received a fair share of advertisements and catalogs.

I HATE GIFT CERTIFICATES. To me, it's a cop-out for the December 24th "Bah Humbug" shopper. Now let's say you want to give your Uncle Joe a present. He's a nice guy, but you don't know him that well. Do you hand him an envelope with a gift certificate to a store he may not like? It just screams, "Last minute – had to get you something and move on!" Why not take a minute... You know he has a sense of humor. K-Mart had that pure silk holiday tie or The Smithsonian catalog had one picturing old ballparks, like Fenway and Wrigley... You do know he likes baseball. Then again, if the K-Mart tie plays fifteen holiday songs and lights up, it may be a tough choice.

The skeptic will ask, "Why not shop online or use QVC or Amazon?" Well... I'm a dinosaur and have bad luck along those lines. With QVC, I ordered two things and sent one back since it didn't perform as easily as was demonstrated on TV. My problem with Amazon is all the collateral and frustrating screens it throws at me. Just send me my stuff and leave me alone!

To me, the sheer variety of things available in catalogs, from military medals to Russian Army surplus, is amazing. Come on! Isn't there someone you know who needs a gas mask?

If you're Irish, there are several catalogs that specialize in clothing, glassware, jewelry and all sorts of stuff made in Ireland or covered with Irish/Celtic legends and lore.

You can run the gamut from the old standbys, like Miles Kimball, Carol Wright Gifts, Lillian Vernon and their sub-companies, to the slightly higher-end Coldwater Creek, and on up to the top-of-the-line Hammacher Schlemmer. There are still store-related catalogs from Lane Bryant and Victoria Secret too.

There are museum catalogs, and several PBS television stations offer a variety of products, including some of their programming from yesterday and yesteryear. It seems that every television show that ever existed is now, or soon will be, available on DVD.

continued

Certain catalogs specialize in hobbies. If, for instance, you ever take up golf... DUCK! Once the word gets around, friends, relatives and casual acquaintances will be ordering you club covers that you'll have to sneak off once you leave the house, gadgets to count your score and calculate the distance to the next hole, and towels with "cute" sayings to wipe your hands, your clubs and your balls.

It still pays to compare prices. There is often a price difference on the same item from one catalog to the next. Sometimes an upscale catalog will charge dramatically more than others, but in that same catalog there maybe an item so unique that it's available nowhere else. On rare occasion, you may find an item cheaper in a store, but usually it is just the opposite. A party supply store may offer a single item that I can buy a dozen of from the Oriental Trading Company for the same price.

But the other day I did buy a mini-tool set at a dollar store for $1.25 and saw the same item in a catalog the next day on sale for $4 and free shipping.

Another example of the price war between catalogs would be the Angel-abra Carousel. That's the little Christmas decoration that holds four candles and when you light them it turns the blades above, which in turn swings the angels around, causing the little metal pipes hanging below to strike two bells until it drives you crazy and you blow out the candles. I remember them growing up in the '50s and I've never seen one actually used. Anyway, it was on sale in one catalog for $3.49, marked down from $4.99. Extra candles were $2.59, marked down from $3.99. The same item in other nostalgic catalogs can run as high as $12.99.

Catalogs are not immune to inflation either. One that used to advertise, "All items in this catalog are $9.99," now features the same items from $14.99 to $19.99 with "many items as low as $9.99."

Each season the various companies search for an exclusive for their catalog. A favorite theme for these items seems to be folk art. This sort of Americana (usually made in China) offers a variety of crudely assembled products, in an appeal to celebrate our forefathers and a time when life was simpler and, apparently, they had problems nailing two boards together. Snowmen also seem to be in vogue. Which leads me to ask the important question, do the children of China make snowmen?

Toy catalogs come in a wide variety of styles and focuses, but most seem to imply that if you buy from them you will have a genius when he or she finishes playing with their products. They seem to flatter the parents as much as engage the child. Whether that's true or not, I don't know... I personally never mastered the yo-yo, much less the gyroscope.

Shall we pause a moment and try to count the number and variety of items that are from Thomas Kinkade, also known as "the Painter of Light?" The man must have never slept! Forget paintings and prints... If it wasn't nailed down or moved slowly enough past him, he slapped some beautiful scene on it and made it available to you.

I must confess, I love fiber optic items. If the fiber optic Christmas tree didn't have that nasty purple cycle, there would be one in this house. Just the other year, I gave one fortunate nephew a fiber optic Indian head that I found in a catalog. It seems they have the technology, but don't know how to apply it evenly. So we get the extremes: from beautiful to tacky.

I'M UNCOMFORTABLE though with some of the items available in catalogs. Actually, there are some things that downright scare me. I don't care for pet gravestones that can be personalized with your former pet's name atop a few cheesy lines of poetry. Is that what you thought of your friend? And besides, not all pets turn out great.

Along that same line of thought, I find the "Uncle Frank" ornaments to be something I'd rather not deal with. You know the ornaments I'm talking about? The one with a frame into which you slide a picture of the recently departed loved one. His name and dates are personalized below the frame and then the company has a few lines they have divined from the grave of Uncle Frank or maybe John Edwards helped them. Either way, Uncle Frank apologizes for not being there in person, but he is there living on in our hearts. Personally, I'd rather remember Uncle Frank in my heart and mind sitting in the recliner, laughing and playing with me on his knee, and showing me how my new toy worked, not hanging from a branch of my tree.

GOURMET FOODS ARE ANOTHER POPULAR CATALOG ITEM from such companies as Figi's, Swiss Colony and The Popcorn Factory. Here we are offered a variety of meats, cheeses, candies and popcorn creations in attractive tins, boxes, jars and towers, for a wide range of prices.

This might be a good place to mention catalog photography. It is an art form, making items seem appealing and larger than life. I would caution you to read the description, especially the weight and size of the containers, then balance that with the price. Get a ruler or check your cabinet to see if it's a good value. Otherwise, you might be disappointed when it arrives at your door.

Recently, I received a catalog from a company called "Wolferman's." It claims to have "a tradition of Fine Food Since 1888." Okay... Without editorial comment, you can get item #5173, called a "Grand Peace on Earth Tower." Here's its description:

A grand tower of inspiration to share and enjoy! Inspired by the dove of peace, your grand gift keeps on giving with five blue boxes of bountiful cheer. Inside, they'll discover Original and Multi-Grain & Honey Signature English Muffins; Cranberry Citrus English Muffin Bread; Raspberry and Blueberry Crumpets; San Francisco Sourdough Miniature English Muffins; Apple Strudel Tea Bread; Tiffin Blend Coffee; a jar of our delicious Pear Butter, and scrumptious French Vanilla Cocoa. Net. Wt. 5lbs 12oz. $49.95.

continued

That's a whopping $8.69/lb... For what? English muffins!

I am a target for many of these catalogs, and so are you if you're over sixty and have a "hanker'n" to relive or share your past. Many of us seem to love the candy we ate, the games we played or the music we listened to. And it's all there waiting for you – for a price. How about fifty-seven hours of World War II movies and documentaries on DVD for $22.00 or the "World's Greatest Polkas" on CD, featuring Laurence Welk and Myron Floren? My Mom used to love Laurence Welk. Ah one – ah two – ah three.

During my time, I have gone from 78s to 45s to EPs to LPs to 8-tracks to cassettes to CDs to whatever is next, and over the years I've purchased the "Top 10 Hits of…" and "The Best of…" What is it today? "The Essential…" You fill in the name of your favorite singer or musician. It gives new life to our memories and we're willing to pay the price to recapture the past.

MAYBE WE'RE FEELING A TAD UNDER THE WEATHER, but not enough to go to the doctor. There's a catalog that can bring us a remedy without leaving the house, from vitamins to pill boxes to quilted air conditioner covers. They're a stamp, a phone call or a few taps on a keyboard away. They're for sale in a catalog, so they must work, these things that help you up, keep you up, push things up, push things in, make you comfortable, make you better, relax you, soothe you, massage you, make things easier to put on, and make it so you don't have to stretch or bend.

Catalogs can also bring you another chance to buy that item "as seen on TV." In case you didn't jot down the number, you can still get that flower-shaped egg poacher for only $5.00. It's that poacher with a "cheerful flower shape" that "harkens back to old England," lest you mix it up with other potential poacher purchases.

These items are all available to help us cook or clean and do things that we want to believe will help make our lives easier. Here too let us pay homage to choppers throughout history, from the Chop-o-matic and those that may have been before to today's Stainless Food Chopper. The modern person has saved so many hours in the kitchen with this handy device that they have had time to relax and watch the paid programming available right now on several local channels.

Today's catalogs bring us a huge assortment of items and, at the risk of boring the reader, I would like to highlight just a few in case, heaven forbid, you threw your allotment of catalogs in the garbage.

The Produce Freshness Disk, available in a package of two for $9.00, promises to help you win the race against time to save your lettuce from going brown, your

pears from rotting and your greens from wilting. The active ingredient in these disks is the same that the produce industry has used for years to eliminate ethylene gas, the ripening gas given off by produce. Hey! Wait a minute! Isn't that one of the potential fuel sources to run my car?

Keeping on with the "disk" theme, the Brown Sugar Disk is available from Starcrest at 2 for $2.00 or on sale from Miles Kimball at $2.59 each. These little ceramic wonders keep your brown sugar fresh after opening and are re-usable. I'm not a baker, but I question how big the market is for this item. Does it work with both light brown sugar and dark brown sugar? And aren't you going to miss pounding that box on the edge of the counter?

Then in the ongoing battle against ethylene gas (see above), we have the E.G.G. (Ethylene Gas Guardian). These last for three months and are only 2 for $5.00, protecting you in their own special way from "black bananas, rotten peaches and fuzzy berries." My God, no! Not fuzzy berries! Let me buy two and call me in the morning.

And so it goes with the new LED items, like the Light-up LED Mug, and the Wacky Chicken that does the chicken dance while the melody plays and that squawks when you hold him by the neck.

Some catalogs have whole sections devoted to farting items. From the Farting Santa to Pull the Finger, how better to remember your loved one this holiday season?

O N THE DAY I STARTED WRITING THIS EPIC, I received seven catalogs and a special offer from the Danbury Mint. It must really be a special offer because this is the third one I've gotten. There was the above-mentioned Wolferman's catalog (the one with the English muffins), Miles Kimball, Young Explorers, The Smithsonian, Current (selling labels, checks and more), Support Plus and Catalog Favorites. This last one features items from several different catalogs, in case you missed them or are not yet on their mailing list.

If you want it, think you want it, or didn't yet know it existed – Wait! It will be in your mailbox tomorrow. And hurry! Time is running out, unless you want to pay for express shipping.

The Little Angel

THE LITTLE ANGEL LAY UPON A SMALL PUFFY CLOUD in the corner of the sky. With her elbows to the edge and hands tucked under her chin, she leaned over to see what was going on below.

Through the fog and smog, through the rain and snow, through rays of sunshine she surveyed the world in preparation. Calendars switched from November to December and, beyond the everyday, she saw a controlled panic become part of some people's disposition.

Planning and execution from decorating to gift buying, all jumbled through the land. The winter wind pushed autumn down the street and the angel saw the world change from yellow and brown to red and green.

Stores and yards began to echo the different stories of the season with constructions, lights and inflations. Wreathes were hung on doors while evergreens and empty spidery branches were refilled with twinkling star-like imitations. The world as the sun went down became a reflection of the nighttime sky.

LOOKING CAREFULLY, the little angel saw snow-covered fields become cluttered with aimless paths created during the many noisy, wonderful snowmen constructions. Tracks appeared on pristine hills as saucers, flyers and toboggans flew into the valleys below.

Cars and people skidded and slipped as much to the right and left as they moved forward, and little tots and unsteady skaters found that other direction as they viewed their friends and the world from an unexpected position.

The angel smiled as the lights from houses grew brighter, as gaily decorated trees and little ceramic villages spilled warmth through their windows and the spirit of giving and sharing and doing was again in season for everyone. Fireplaces burned, not only for their warmth, but also for the clustered family, telling stories, talking and sharing memories they somehow forgot to do all year-round.

Some people stagger through the snow, not only for the bargains in the stores, but to their houses of worship. Prayers, songs and carols mix with scripture to tell the real reason for the chaos. The glory of a housewife-soprano tears at the heart and the gentle voices of the children's choir pushes tears over the brim as the congregation remembers those absent from the celebration.

THE LITTLE ANGEL MOTIONS TO OTHERS in the clouds and each peeks down at his or her world and smiles at the love rising throughout the land. Each tries their best to comfort those below, silently imploring them to remember happy times and urging them to enjoy their life, to forget petty problems, to forgive, to love, to hug, to laugh and smile through tears and try to carry these feelings past the season. This chorus in the sky, just hiding from our view, just out of reach, offers no great solutions to the world's problems. It merely urges faith, belief and understanding. They know the limits our minds set on us, but if each year we could renew our love and take a small step more in kindness...

It may not solve or make understandable all the cruelties and injustice in the world, and we may only be able to give a dollar extra to charity, but other things don't cost anything more. Can I forgive my neighbor for doing something I didn't like? Can I try to understand that a homeless person may not be a criminal, but truly an unfortunate soul who has fallen through the cracks?

So many questions in life, so few black and white answers... Wouldn't it be nice to be able to lead with the heart and not be afraid to leave it there, exposed?

Balsam Boss

With red nose and Red Rose
she urges the late shift on.
Weavers of branch and wire
race the November clock to December.
Ribbons and cones
added to wreath and garland
as the winter season grows.

Hard taskmaster, cheerleader –
Orders made ready
to where cold weather
is somewhat a novelty –
Or maybe for someone
just down the road –
It must look like the picture.

Ten-inch or sixteen-inch,
a few oddball flavors.
Foot upon foot of needle chain
to hang on a door,
to wrap lamp post and rail.
An added touch, another bow.
Pull them tight, tie them right.

Just a few more weeks,
a flurry leading to celebration.
Seasonal elves, keep the life spirit.
Your magic from the north
brings happiness and warmth,
from a child's wonder
to an old man's smile.

Another Winter Ditty

With fireplaces to cuddle close to,
snow to soften every sound,
with rosy red and evergreen
whether real or artificial.

With familiar carols being sung,
smiles from someone dear,
with memories all tangled up,
good times added once a year.

We think of kings and stars
or chimneys and St. Nick,
giving or getting or celebrating
on Merry Christmas Day.

The year to come,
let it be good to you,
with all the seasons full
of what you're looking for.

Winter Recipe

Take a field surrounded by evergreens under moonlight, covered with a fresh coating of snow. (Optionally, sprinkle in a cottage with lights showing through the windows and smoke rising from the chimney.)

Add a Festival of Lights, celebrating an ancient story of the miracle of the oil, complete with candle-lighting, prayers, games and presents.

Mix a healthy supply of house decorating with lights, bows, inflatables, wreathes, stars and symbols. (There can be no excess.)

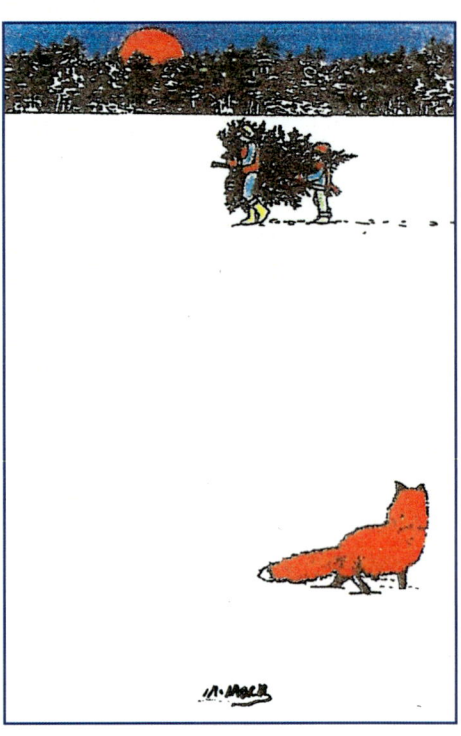

Stir with shopping for gifts for family and friends to help make them happy, and you too for the giving.

Fluff with a warm fire (or your best imitation) inside your home and surround it with more decorations, family and friends.

Sprinkle the mix with caroling, visiting Santa, wrapping, tagging and hiding gifts. Get carried away with the pace. Give into it all. Buy it all.

Set the oven. Prepare for the meal. Trim the tree with memories, happy, new, old, laugh and cry as each year you build your tree into a tacky, cluttered, wonderful symbol of what you and your family are.

Then stop, think and celebrate the birth, the cause of it all. See the star in your life and hold it close to your heart. As close as you hold your wife, your husband, your Mom, your Dad, your children, even Grandpa and Grandma and Aunt So-and-So.

When done, it serves a multitude and hopefully will carry you through a cold hard winter and into spring.

What Must They Think of Us?

What kind of life do they lead?
What must they think of us?
These always–happy winter people,
these people who sit on a bench day and night –
The smiling skaters, the old couple strolling along,
the boy and girl who wave to us first thing in the morning.
Are they happy with the attention they get?
Watching the train pass through,
looking at giants for only a month or two.
How many songs can the carolers sing?
It seems the children never finish their snowman
and the young boy's thirst at the fountain is never quenched.
Each night we leave them in the dark.
They are accessories to our lives.
It won't be long before the hibernation.
Not only will we turn out the lights
in their snow-covered porcelain homes,
but we'll wrap them in blankets of tissue
and layer them in labeled containers,
carrying them into the solitude of the attic –
These little people, these resin people.
What must they think of us?

The Celebration

Santa Claus, the Easter Bunny, the Tooth Fairy and Jesus Christ

When I was young, I was taught to believe in
Santa Claus, the Easter Bunny, the Tooth Fairy and Jesus Christ.
When I grew up and got married and had children,
I became three of them and still believe in the other.

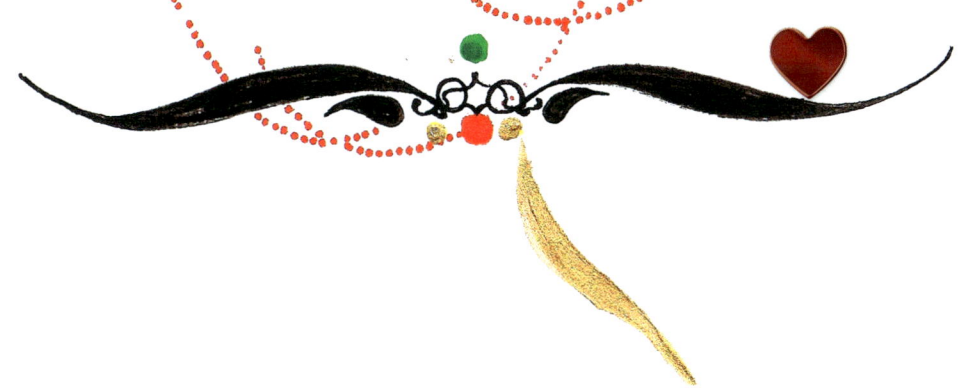

Well, Just So You Know...

Well, just so you know...
I've harvested the plastic forest,
spread out the wrinkled garland,
and put each memory in place.
Frosty the salesman and I
have shared our bounty
and it is wrapped in color,
waiting for that special morning.
I'm soaking in the carols.
They echo through the house.
The snowballs play
their seasoned songs.
The lights blink in the kitchen
and hold on tight outdoors.
The cats are posing with the
Santa frog under the bush.
I look to the mail each day
for friends' greetings
and Scrooge's accounting
of what's been spent.
I wish this time would continue.
Throughout the year, we could have
cranberry days and eggnog nights,
runny noses and rosy cheeks.
We could have giving and
sharing and loving and
stars and stories and tinsel
and candles and... and... and...

Listen! Do You Hear?

Listen! Do you hear?
Starting just a little while ago
and lasting for a month or so,
coming from radios, TVs, MP3s,
coming from iPods, CD players
and countless other devices,
record players, cassette players,
8-tracks – Ha! – Your heart.
It's carols and songs,
Christmas and winter.
They're wonderful and corny.
They're beautiful and familiar.
They're for kids.
They're for me and you.
As you hear them,
you smile and laugh. Your youth...
You pause and think
of the Christmas story,
of the choir of people in your heart.
Friends to your ears appear –
Rudolf, Frosty, Charlie Brown,
angels, wise men, the Christ child.
And so as you prepare
to give and celebrate,
the soundtrack, the background,
drifts on the chilling air
to comfort and entertain
as you wrap and worship
and then, before you know it,
your off-key voice is silenced.
Though many are winter songs,
they all seem to end late on the 25th
or early on the 26th.
Put away before the decorations –
Shelved for eleven months,
as the wrapping paper is tossed
and the batteries are added,
collecting dust, fading from our mind
till next year, just after Thanksgiving.
What's your favorite?

# To Celebrate Christmas

You need:

A huge quantity of boxes in the attic filled with:

- an artificial tree (directions either lost or in a foreign tongue)
- artificial garland (shedding)
- a wide assortment of ornaments (tacky and sentimental)
- a manger (w/Joseph, Mary, Baby Jesus, 3 kings, 2 shepherds, animals optional)
- indoor and outdoor lights (must be tangled w/bulb out in each string)
- a miniature village (church non-denominational and villagers ethnically balanced)
- assorted Xmas novelties and music globes (plastic, resin, fiber optic – all cutting edge)
- leftover boxes and wrapping paper (tags and tape lost)
- several tree toppers (variations of angels and stars)
- matted and lumpy cotton snow.

A list of:

- who to invite and when (explore once again the land mine of family relations)
- what to cook (over-buy, over-cook and hold your breath)
- what to buy for whom (believe that Uncle Bill will like that tie).
  NOTE: Children – No Limits

Decorate:

- Do as you've always done (see above).
- Then add more to see how fast you can make Reddy Kilowatt run.

Buy:

- Hit the mall running.
- Thumb through the catalogues and turn down the pages.
- Make the "plastic" melt.

Wrap:

- Mix up the paper.
- Include the batteries.
- Try to remember where everything is that you bought.
- Then after wrapping, find new places to hide them.
- Did you tag everything?

Weather:

- Should be brisk to cold.
- Add snow for caroling and Christmas Eve, melting from roads and sidewalks as needed.

Events:

- Christmas tree lightings (come with "ahhs").
- Christmas caroling (even if you sing off-key).
- Take a ride to see other decorations. (Steal ideas for next year.)
- Have a sing-along.

Misc.

- Note: The person who recorded the dog barking "Jingle Bells" is probably a millionaire.

The Story:

- Same as last year. God loved us so much – Gave his only son – It's his birthday – Can be added to above or take the place of all of the above.

The feeling:

- Better to give than to receive.
- Love, family, church and a wealth of memories.

Penalties for peeking:

- Ravioli wrists, linguini lips, and continual nightmares involving Gabby Hayes, Pat Buttram, Tonto and Robin.

It's a Celebration

Ring the bells.
Play the music.
It's a celebration!

Decorate the houses.
Put up the tree.
It's a celebration!

Sing the carols.
Buy the presents.
It's a celebration!

Don't be afraid.
Enjoy the holiday.
It's a celebration!

The child is born.
The children are happy.
It's a celebration!

Our neighbor is forgiven.
Our family is close.
It's a celebration!

We miss the ones gone.
We cherish their memory.
We celebrate them too...

Give up our hearts.
Enjoy the giving.
It's a celebration!

Don't stand still.
Don't "Bah Humbug" the day.
It's a celebration!

Giving, giving, giving –
Your heart, your self.
It's a celebration!

Plan the get-together.
Do the shopping.
It's a celebration!

Find the sales.
Remember those?
It's a celebration!

Wrap and ribbon,
light and swag.
Boost the celebration.

Gaudy or tasteful,
stranger or friend.
Find the celebration.

Feel good in doing.
Risk a smile.
It's a celebration!

Teach warm hearts.
Look for no reward.
It's a celebration!

And try, try, try
to carry it past
the celebration.

Holiday Memories

Have some? Good? Bad?
How do you remember them?
A soldier set, an electric train,
snowy footsteps from the fireplace?
People working hard for my happiness
from a plastic Corvette to a puppy,
up late trimming the tree
turning the bad side to the wall.
Up early struggling with the meal,
making it all seem normal.

That young man so worldly
he worships only an aluminum tree.
It's a day off from a busy time,
sending gifts from far away.
Awkward ages with no real guide.
Everything is disjointed, out of sync.
It's still red and green and snow-covered,
but lots of things are not cool.
You try to be cool, man,
but mostly you're just alone.

Then comes the beautiful scary discovery.
A love found and stories with meaning,
the conscious and unconscious beginnings,
new traditions blended with old,
new generations building memories –
Doing it wrong, doing it right –
For no reason, for the right reason –
Crowding the table for all to come.
Giving with heart and pocketbook.
Learning to give and accept thanks,
and to appreciate something that doesn't fit.

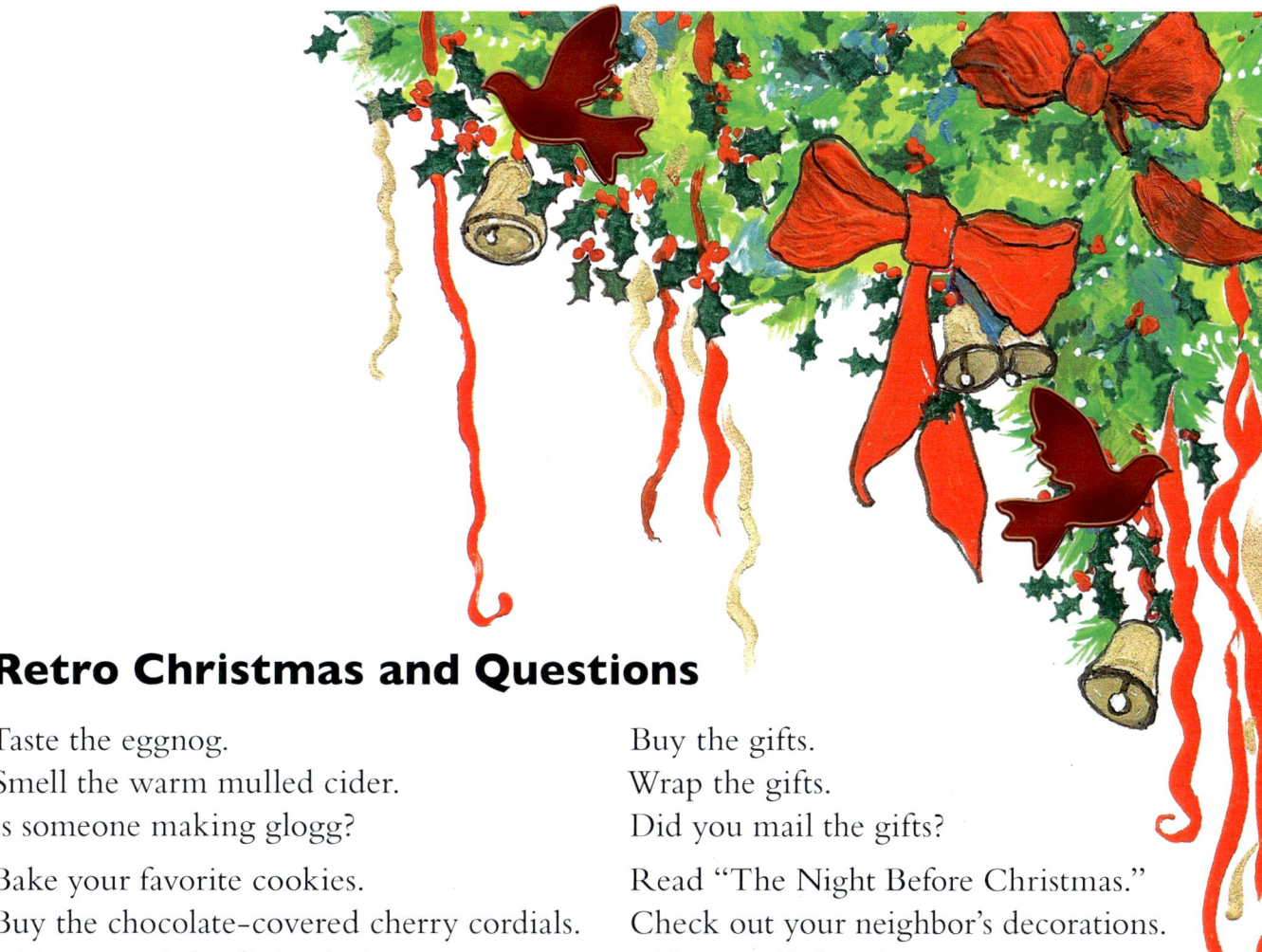

Retro Christmas and Questions

Taste the eggnog.
Smell the warm mulled cider.
Is someone making glogg?

Bake your favorite cookies.
Buy the chocolate-covered cherry cordials.
Did you mail the fruitcake?

Ribbon candy, Thin Mints,
candy canes, chocolate Santas –
Do you have an orange for the stocking?

Bubble lights, old-fashioned lights,
popcorn and cranberry garland –
Do you place or throw your tinsel?

Glass and plastic ornaments,
clear and multicolor lights –
Angel or star atop your tree?

Buy the gifts.
Wrap the gifts.
Did you mail the gifts?

Read "The Night Before Christmas."
Check out your neighbor's decorations.
Did you tell *the* Christmas story?

Cherish the memories.
Try to make new ones.
Do you feel the warmth of the season?

Sing the carols.
Ring the bells.
Did you relish all the sights and smells?

The Christmas Card

The Christmas card sadly is going.
What once took two deliveries a day
now is sent by only a few.
I once sold them with wrapping paper –
An old memory from so many years ago.
My Mom used to write a whole bundle.
She'd sit on her bed and address them.
Then for some she'd get chatty.
This was a chance to touch base
with more than a few
to tell them what's happened
and that she loved them too.
To some, she'd send a delicate hankie
and the old maid aunt would smile.
It was and is a time of communication.
People who you know as friends,
whose lives have wandered different roads –
The relatives, aunts, uncles, all the rest.
Some send stories of all their travels
and their children's awards and accomplishments.
Others have their name printed,
stamp it, put in the mail –
Their job is done.
Still others send photos of their kids,
their pets, their kids and their pets,
their whole family, the pets and a neighbor's kid.
Me? Well, I love to send them.
I pick cards I'd love to get
and then run through the Christmas list.

Mostly I just say, "Love Dave,"
but as I go down the list
each name brings back a memory —
Old neighbors, old friends,
friends close in hard times
but now spread thin,
relatives who you could let go,
but I don't want to —
Groups you work with
or where you used to work,
and you wonder how many are still there.
Add to that those you see every day.
For some, I add a poem,
something from my family's tradition.
A new one each year —
A friend makes them lovely
and I just have to worry about enough postage.
Like the whole season,
it's a chance to spread love to your world,
to appreciate the meaning of, for me,
Christmas, Chanukah, love and friendship —
Oh, how hard to lessen the list —
I've lost someone dear.
How happy to add a name,
a new friend or relative,
an old friend found, new family.
I guess it's a capsule,
part of the traditions of the past,
a current engaging happening
and setting foundations for the future.
Of course, you could send an e-card.

Love
Dave

Some Christmas Wishes and Questions

May your snowman melt at night, in February.

May Santa hear all your wishes and not all your words.

When you pull on his beard, may it bring a smile to his face and yours.

May you see the Christmas star on a night when you are at peace.

May all your Christmas lights light the first time.

Try to put the crèche in a better place than the lighted porcelain house.

May all your old ornaments and memories be unbroken.

Try to squeeze in time to enjoy the season and all that it means.

May your fiber optic snowman not fool around
with your neighbor's wooden reindeer.

May you be warmed by the light of children's eyes on Christmas morning.

May your Christmas train stay on its tracks
and bring delight to the old man's heart.

Here's hoping the star or angel on top is straight, even if the tree is not.

May you string more popcorn than you eat.

If you see Santa before Christmas, put in a good word for me.

If you love snow, may it fall all over your world.

If you love Christmas, may the snow fall on Christmas Eve,
but leave the sidewalks clear.

May you remember all the words to the carols – "like a light bulb!"

May you sing all season loudly, with gusto, with feeling,
and occasionally on-key.

May your cocoa always have marshmallows.

May you be warm in your mittens and your heart.

Don't give because you have to, give because you want to.

Try to tell the Christmas story and throw in the miracle of light –
Old and New Testament often complement each other.

Store up all the love and warmth of Christmas because January and February can be very long and very cold and the batteries can run low on your new toys and your brother or sister may not share, or some of your clothes may not fit even if they are the right size (which means you ate too much for the holidays and the stationary bike has been too stationary), and it gets dark early so that everything seems gray or brown or dark blue.

May the clear, cold sky on a bright winter night give you insight to a new day.

May your tree be a hodgepodge of color and memories
or a solid color of your choosing. Your choice.

May Santa's elves get more than minimum wage.

When you tell a Christmas story, try to be a child at heart. You should get as much enjoyment telling it as your listeners get hearing it.

May your tree's bare spot always be toward the wall.

Who a gift is to should always be more important than who it is from.

If you decorate competitively, good luck?

May you never run short of batteries or patience on Christmas morning.

Young parents should not be discouraged if the child has more fun
with the paper than the gift.

Don't fret if you find some decoration after you've put everything else away. Just think of it as an early start on next year.

If you're too tired to put Christmas decorations away, try dressing Santa as the Easter Bunny.

If you hear prancing on your roof, make sure it's not squirrels in your attic.

When's the last time you wore a kerchief or hat to bed?

Fluffing

"FLUFFING" IS A GENERAL TERM in my family that applies to the required preparation of the Christmas tree between purchase or un-boxing till it is ready for lights and ornamentation.

With a live tree you have the thrill of fastening it to the family car or SUV without scratching the paint or having it relocating itself to the side of the road half-way home.

Upon arrival home, you put it in water and hope it doesn't freeze while you prepare to deal with it.

If you haven't cut it yourself at a tree farm, you're supposed to make a fresh cut across the bottom of the trunk. The saw is either in the cellar or the shed and the blade is usually dull after a year of pruning. Once you have retrieved the saw, you make your "straight" cut and the fun now begins.

From the attic, three different Christmas tree stands appear, each a technological improvement over the last and all missing at least one piece, lost somewhere in the dark and dusty attic or recycled almost a year ago with a wad of used wrapping paper.

After a brief trip to the local box store, you return with the latest tree stand variation, not much better than a nail sticking out of a couple pieces of wood.

The tree is squeezed through the door, leaving a small trail of broken branches and needles. It is at this time you remember how, as a Boy Scout, you used sap to glue things together.

Hopefully the trunk isn't too wide for the stand and you screw the three thumbscrews tight. With a smile you climb out from under the tree, only to watch it slowly tilt over and leave a wonderfully long streak on the painted wall. You climb back under the tree with an assortment of bricks, stones, dictionaries and coffee table books to help keep the tree pointing toward the ceiling.

Water is added and you work at keeping that water in the stand, which means harsh words to curious pets and children.

And for you artificial tree owners? You have separated the tree box from other boxes and plastic tubs containing the balance of your Christmas decorations. You have opened the box and removed the stand. Next you remove the first section of trunk and insert it in the stand and either sort through the color-coded branches and mount them onto said trunk or if you have pre-attached limbs, let them fall into place.

You then put the tree skirt around the stand or, if you have a tree like my first artificial tree, you remove the color-coded branches, remove the trunk from the stand, add the skirt you forgot to put on first, and then reinsert the first trunk section followed by the branches. With color-coded branches, time and frustration sometimes widens or destroys the holes in the trunk and re-drilling is a new step in the tree's assembly.

The second section now follows, as you grapple over the lower section to find the hole to insert your growing evergreen. Finally the top clump is attached and... Behold!

WHAT COMES NEXT is universal to trees, live or artificial. A chorus of supervisors or experts tells you the tree is not straight and what you can or should do about it. These people appear from nowhere and you just happen to be related to each and every one of them. Where they were during your earlier struggles with the tree is not discussed, but at this point it's easier to try and please them.

The first order of business is to find the good side of the tree. This is accomplished by finding the worst side (gaping holes and the like) and turning it to the wall or your neighbor's house through the window.

Next we deal with the word "straight" (up and down, that is). The commentators and the critics are sitting (comfortably) in assorted locations around the room. What works for one does not always work for the other. Tempers are strained a bit and the holiday spirit takes a brief "time out."

Finally it is in place and all are satisfied until they reappear to lend guidance in the spacing of lights and decorations.

With a live tree, a time is given for the tree to settle and find its adjustments to the indoor climate. This is a natural "fluffing."

The artificial tree takes manual intervention. You bought this baby because it was full and looked real. Now is when you really pay the price. Crammed into a box for ten or eleven months, you must bring it back to life. Letting it sit for a day is not going to help. You must fluff each branch to its three, four or five-point best. You must bend branches to be at their fullest and make your first attempt to cover the myriad gaps that appear.

If you are lucky, the supervisors are out of the room. But with your luck they hit the couches, chairs and recliners for Round Two of helpful suggestions. With a smile, you look about you and consider bringing all the presents back, changing religions and writing some of the dear loves out of your will.

continued

At this point, pet owners should consider anchoring the tree to the wall so that Kitty will do minimal damage when she decides to take an Olympic vertical jump toward the heirloom ornament on the topmost branch. Now dash away all! Or Rover gets into the "holiday spirit" and starts wagging his tail and diving in for a drink of flavored water or, God help you, to mark his territory.

W E MAKE THESE "FLUFFING" CEREMONIES yearly and eventually embrace our critics in the spirit of the season. It becomes as much a part of Christmas as the star on top of the tree and the story of Christ's birth. In the end, we untangle the wad of lights and find the burned out bulb. The gifts get bought and wrapped, the meals get cooked, and we embrace our loved ones with a heart full of "Merry Christmas" and "Happy New Year."

The Christmas Card II

I have arrived.
I have been opened.
You hold me in your hands.
Your eyes feast upon my winter scene
or on a gap-toothed youth saying, "Cheese!"
Inside are the wishes,
perhaps a few personal words
and a name –
Or "Love" and a name.
A friend, a cousin, a brother, a lover,
a child's scrawl with letters headed in different directions,
somebody from work, a neighbor,
people from the past, parents, children,
your newspaper boy looking for a tip,
the formally printed Family So-and-So.
They've taken the time.
They've felt the obligation.
They're full of the season
whatever the reason
behind those Santas, those snowmen,
those snow-covered fields with barren trees,
those little ones trapped in
red velvet dresses and alpine shorts,
those pictures of the birthday boy in his manger
or angels floating above stained glass windows.
Behind all that there is one wonderful fact.
You are a part of their lives.
Rejoice! Make sure they're in your heart too.

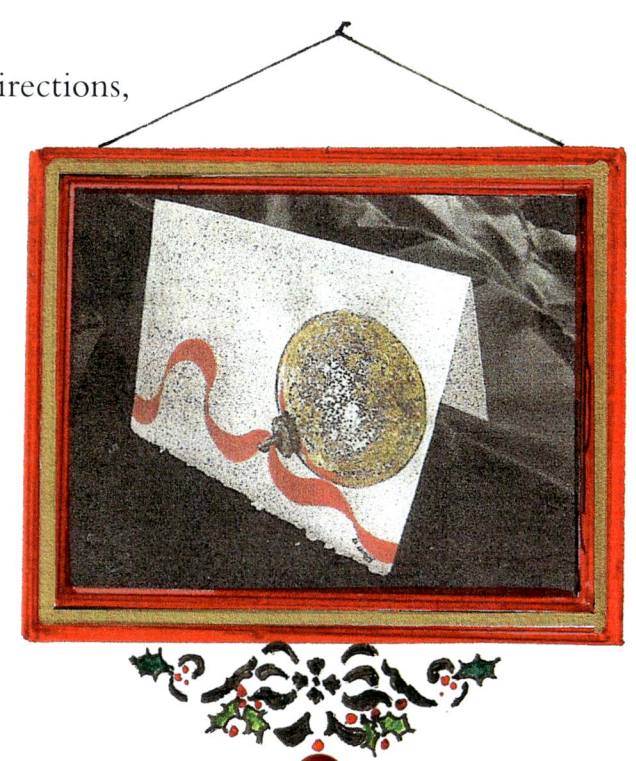

The Hodgepodge Tree

IF YOU ARE ONE THAT IS THEMED AND PERFECTLY NEAT, if you deal in single colors and balance, turn away, turn away quick.

My tree these last thirty years has been artificial, inadequately fluffed and covered from head to toe (or top to stand) with a hodgepodge of ornaments and lights.

I grew up with real cut trees. Balsam was what we could afford, bad side to the wall, Noma angel on top with tinsel (lead and cellophane), big lights and child-eyed ornaments of all colors and shapes. Unscrew the bulb, put in the aluminum reflector, screw the bulb back in and move to the next. It was all a wonder, with a Lionel train from Mom and Pa (Grandpa), a big plastic Corvette from my brother, a soldier set and a one-night struggle putting up the tree. All these people, in my reflection, worked to make my growing up Christmas' happy and special.

Single and away from home, I had a (*shudder, shudder*) tabletop aluminum tree. Sending gifts home and to nieces and nephew, I don't think I was a very good shopper then.

Years pass and then came my life's love and, as they say, new traditions were about to begin. The first married Christmas and a little apartment in the center of town. It was our only Christmas alone and without much money it was off to Gloria's and Q-Gardens for an assortment of decorations, the best a little money could buy.

THE YEARS CONTINUE TO PASS until suddenly it's today and I've just finished decorating. Since Thanksgiving, Christmas music plays in the car and throughout the house as different stages of decoration take place. Bushes bowed and lit, a star flown into the tree, a spray of greens for Carol's old sled, pine bows and a few new things. Inside, a small plastic tree for the kitchen window, miniature villages, snow globes (most musical) and a brand-new bubble wreath over the mantle. The tree went up on Friday, the lights on Saturday, that's imitation big old lights and bubble lights, and a wraparound train in the middle.

So today comes the ornaments, boxes and boxes of ornaments. And, as I start unwrapping them, I'm crying and smiling, remembering what has become a "family tree." Sadly, angels have taken on greater meaning and I have no one telling me "a little to the left," but in the same breath, a smile comes with a series of gold-plated Miles Kimball specials, stamped with a year and my children's names. Volume, sheer volume covers gaps and spaces. Beautiful glass ornaments carried home from a vacation, complete with a school picture glued to construction paper and

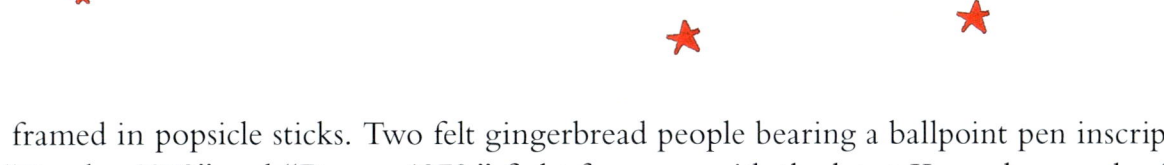

framed in popsicle sticks. Two felt gingerbread people bearing a ballpoint pen inscription, "Carol – 1972" and "Dave – 1972," fight for space with the latest Keepsake wonder from Hallmark. Some bell ornaments from my mother's tree, faded, but still able to ring, stand side-by-side with my kids' annual choices for a new tree decoration.

Branch by branch I hang and clip random groupings to make a grand design. A few of those first ornaments, a bird in a tarnished cage and a mouse from China or Japan, still grace the tree. No ornament is ever thrown away because it's old or of questionable taste, but some literally fall apart or are broken in storage.

The cat is no longer a threat, grown and comfortable in my chair. She watches or sleeps or yells for a little attention. I need not tie the tree to the wall or put unbreakable ornaments on the bottom anymore. I'm free to put the fragile plump purple octopus lady near the bell from the Jimmy Stewart Museum. Everybody join Zuzu, "Teacher says every time a bell rings, an angel gets his wings." And so it goes... Candy canes over a few branches, all the lights working, all the memories there, waiting for someone's nosy look.

HOMEMADE, HANDMADE, MASS-PRODUCED... Each holds something of my past and my love for the holiday. It holds my love for my family and in a special way it is a family tree — silly and sacred traditions lumped on 7½ feet of metal, wire and plastic.

Ornaments

The boxes are down and open,
all in place and waiting,
still hidden in tissue and wrap.
Music playing – Let us begin!
Mine are a colored confusion.
They're red, green, white, blue and gold.
They're not red, green, white, blue or gold.
They're from where we've been –
From big stores, little stores.
They're machine-made.
They're handmade by skilled hands.
They're handmade by little hands.
They're handmade by loving hands.
They come from China, Japan, Taiwan,
from Europe and the U.S.A.
They come from Central Grammar,
Point Beach and Calf Pen Meadow.
Made of glass, crystal, plastic,
felt, doilies and popsicle sticks –
They don't hang in any order,
except for two together.
It's all about filling gaps.
It's all about remembering.
It's all about our love and family.

Tinsel

WHEN I WAS YOUNG, we had a reasonable number of decorations for our tree. It was a live tree and we had the traditional struggles of putting it in the stand and turning the bad side toward the wall. A little bit of a discussion then ensued before we could get everyone to agree on what "straight" was and how to get there. Then you added water, the dog drank the water, and so you added some more.

Now the reason you had a live tree was because artificial trees were not generally available or invented yet. Yes, I'm that old...

You'd go to a tree lot and watch the ritual proceed. First of all, if there was another kind of tree, other than a balsam, I wasn't aware of it. That was the only type of tree we could afford. The guy would pull a tree off the ropes, shake it a little, lift it and pound it on the ground. Assuming we weren't knee-deep in needles, the price would be negotiated, and the tree tied onto the roof or the front fender of our 1936 black Dodge sedan.

Our decorations consisted of a blonde angel in a white dress with silver wings, a small variety of glass ornaments and bells, and two or three sets of standard Noma lights. After testing the bulbs, we unscrewed about half of them and inserted reflectors. Once that was done, we screwed the bulbs back in, retested and started wrapping them around the tree.

Angel, lights, then ornaments and finally we added the tinsel. Some of the more adventurous families had snow applied to the branch tips with either a spray can or a Lux or Ivory Snow concoction.

The application of the tinsel was the most important element of the decoration process. It could make or break how the tree finally looked. Now I'm sure the tinsel was made of or contained lead to start with, and I'm sure I and every little kid of that era put some in his or her mouth, and I know the pets ate it because what they didn't swallow they would arrange nicely on the living room rug, along with half of their dinner.

I don't want to put down science, but I'm still alive and everyone I know is either alive or dead, and those that have died did not die from tinsel poisoning that I know. On the other hand, all the pets that I had at that time are dead. For many of them, we don't know the cause of death. But since I'm sixty-five, I don't think any of them would have lasted anyway, except maybe a turtle or a parrot. I didn't have a turtle or a parrot though. I think turtles are dumb pets and a parrot has a limited vocabulary, but that's just my opinion.

THERE ARE CERTAIN RULES for putting tinsel on a tree, and those rules vary from one family to another. At some point in the '50s or '60s, silver metal tinsel was replaced by cellophane tinsel (sometimes in different colors), but the rules were pretty much unchanged.

If you were a baby, you didn't care. Just feed me, clean me and keep me entertained when I'm awake. Maybe the colored lights are interesting for a few minutes, but so is my toe.

continued

When you worked your way up to toddler status, there comes a lot of "No!" "Don't touch!" and "Get that out of your mouth!" Well... Life is to be sampled, isn't it?

If you're lucky though, maybe an older brother or sister or some misguided uncle will let you apply a little tinsel to the tree. For some reason, the shiny things are too high to reach, but at least the bottom deserves some beauty.

This derelict older person shows you how to gently apply a few strands to the end of each branch. Humph! Easy enough... So you grab as much tinsel as you can hold in one little fist and from a distance of about ten inches, you give a stiff-armed throw. Plop! Some actually has found the tree and you look back at the people behind you for their applause and gratitude for your help. They say you're a big boy, but they also move you away from the tree and give you a Christmas cookie.

As you grow older, you are counted on to help decorate, unless Santa does it all on Christmas Eve when the children are nestled in bed. I have found that this only lasts a year or two. Then Santa needs help and the tree goes up earlier and Mom and Dad aren't as grumpy on Christmas morning. The problem at this age is that you "have" to do it, even if you don't want to. So you make a face, grab a bunch of tinsel and throw it toward the top of the tree in hopes of it landing on each branch, just as your parents want. Plop! It doesn't... Over and over it seems you are told how to do it with less patience and some threats as the night grows late.

Finally, as an adult, you know how it works. If you don't have kids, you can do theme trees, single stranding the tinsel and, instead of snow flocking, you might have progressed (if it was invented yet) to using angel hair (not the pasta). This is stretched gently across any big gaps in the tree that you can't cover with long dangling ornaments.

But if you have started a family, then you are part of the earlier tinsel-hanging brigade. Time changes the method and what is ideal varies in direct proportion to how many things you've just finished assembling and how many batteries you've had to scrounge up so everything will work on Christmas morning.

Assuming the wrapping is done, you help the littlest ones put out milk and cookies (or beer and cookies in my house after the first year or two of toy assemblies) and you put the cherubs to bed. The older kids are getting tired and cranky now, and they know the presents are bought, so your threats of what will happen if they don't help or behave are empty. Finally you tell them to go to bed and close the door.

You pick up the tinsel, look at your spouse and throw it at the tree. Plop! It's fine. Let's get the presents out of hiding and under the tree and go to bed so we can get some sleep.

With the dawn's early light comes the jumping-on-the-bed bit and everyone is happy and excited. Mom and Dad, a bit rumpled, lead the way downstairs. The tree is turned on and the unwrapping, in whatever tradition works at your house, begins.

And everything is warm and beautiful as the tinsel reflects the colored lights and moves gently as presents are delivered to their new owners and the Christmas music tells us stories of a birthday or about wonderlands, snowmen and reindeer.

I am...

Bubbling up, bubbling up –
Never down.
Yellow, red, orange, purple, blue –
Never green.
Secured in multicolored bases.
Dare you to keep me straight.
Bubbling up, bubbling up –
Never down.
Sometimes slow to start.
Sometimes I just evaporate.
I take you back
and leave you in the '50s.
Bubbling up, bubbling up –
Check the motion.

Come closer... Come closer!
See all the ornaments around me?
Plastic and glass, paper and tin,
store-bought, homemade
from remember when?
And then, and then and now,
the old, the new technology.
Things spin, change colors
and seem to move about.
Me? Not me... I'm just
bubbling up, bubbling up –
Never down.

The Job

People ask why I stay.
Why keep the job?
What is your future?
Surely you can do better...
Maybe that's true,
I don't know.
Here there is no height discrimination.
I get to use my hands,
my building skills,
from woodworking to plastics to computers.
Over the years I've stayed fresh,
at the top of my game.
My co-workers are my friends.
We smile, laugh and sing
while we build grins and laughter.
Our boss is just us, oversized,
working to bring happiness and joy
to little ones the world wide.
We wear rather unique work clothes
and have a bit of magic up our sleeves.
I won't give it away,
but think "condensed" or "miniaturized..."
How else can everything (everything!)
for all the good little boys and girls
fit in one sack, in one sleigh,
and be light enough for
eight tiny reindeer to pull through the sky?
Just to see all those happy faces
shining on Christmas morning
is bonus enough for me!
Now if you'll excuse me,
this time of year we get a lot of overtime.

Under the Tree

Finally the shopping is done,
things are assembled and wrapped.
You have decorated.
You have taught that giving
is better than receiving.
You have put yourself in debt
so your kids get all they want.
You have told them the Christmas story
and taken them to church and Santa.
Now you collapse into bed.
No visions dance in your head,
but in what seems like a second
little voices echo in and around you.
"Mommy! Daddy! Wake up!
Wake up! It's morning!"
You pop an eye open and
try to focus on the alarm clock.
OK... Technically they're correct,
but you murmur "Too early…"
Those little hands you love so much
tear the bedclothes to the floor
and your mattress becomes a trampoline.
"Come on! Get up! It's Christmas!"
Bodies rise stiffly and robes are donned,
unshaven and unkempt
the loving couple moves forward.

One of you holds back the stampede
while the other stumbles down the stairs.
The tree is lit. The camera is at the ready.
Here comes the culmination
of a season of joy and celebration.
You focus the camera halfway up
and the children seem to pause on cue.
They take in the scene –
Lights, decorations, presents.
"Wow!" The camera snaps
and, as if that were the official restart,
the youngsters finish the race
to what is under the tree!

Scuttle and Buddle

Scuttle and buddle the sight.
Santa's coming tonight!
Sing, you choirs.
Watch for the safest of flyers.
Snow or wind or rain –
It's all just the same.
He fits down any chimney
by cracky or by jiminy.
He does his job so well
that grown-ups can never tell,
but with that smile and that famous wink,
he must be more than a prehistoric link
to a giver of gifts.
I wonder how many children see him as
the head of Heaven out of season.

Tinsel and Pine Needles

It's days past Christmas.
Clothes have been hung or returned,
sweaters paraded in front of the givers,
toys blended with old favorites,
and the floor is covered with tinsel and pine needles.

It's back to work
or residence has been established
on the couch in front of the TV.
Leftovers have all been consumed
and the floor is covered with tinsel and pine needles.

Decorations are boxed and stored,
things returned to their proper positions.
The Christmas spirit has morphed
into New Year's celebrations and resolutions
and you vacuum up the tinsel and pine needles.

What's left besides yesterday's routine?
Did you forget a new set of memories
like that one decoration you find,
usually on the ninth day of July,
with a fresh supply of tinsel and pine needles?

What about the wonder and the why?
The community, the comradeship,
the beauty, the celebration, the giving...
Not that long ago when
the tinsel hung from pine branches with all their needles.

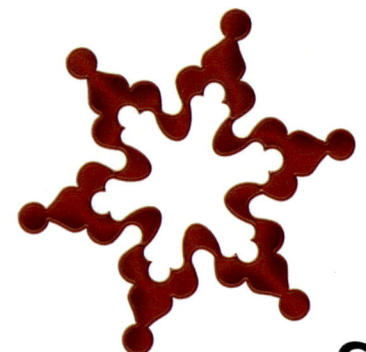

Christmas Numbers

50 sets of 75 C7-sized LED multicolored lights
on four bushes, neatly arranged,
each topped with a GE 100 mini-light ball,
one red, one green, one blue and one white,
followed by two white willow branch deer
outlined with 150 white mini-lights each.
One grazing, one with head raised,
both with heads nodding...
A lamppost wrapped with garland
intertwined with 40 white mini-lights
and one big red bow.
One air-filled Christmas merry-go-round
with lights and snow falling internally.
Two floodlights, one red and one green,
shining on the front of the house.
Manger scene with Joseph, Mary, three Kings,
three camels, one drummer boy, one shepherd,
two sheep, one Frosty, one cow, one donkey,
one angel, one nutcracker, three carolers,
one toy soldier, and one baby Jesus
made of plastic and internally lit.

One white spotlight shining on the front door,
which is decorated to look like a foil-wrapped present.
The cross-shaped ribbon in contrasting color
contains a computer chip in the bow
that is motion-activated and plays 15 carols randomly.
House and roof outlined in multicolor C9 bulbs.
Gutters give birth to 15 strings of white icicle lights
with 100 white mini-lights each, dangling at various lengths.
One "Santa Train" made up of over 800 mini-lights
of red, green and gold blinking to simulate
the train moving and Santa waving.
All this plugged into 24 extension cords totaling 909',
several of these with three outlet endings.
They plug into six timers that in turn plug into three GFI outlets,
one in the front of the house,
one on the side of the house,
one in the back of the house.
One three-day storm with 6.95" of rain,
winds steady at 25 mph with gusts to 50 mph,
and the redecoration includes
one tattered wreath on the door.

That Time
Before Spring Comes

What Will My Winter Be?

Resting with routine,
filling hours easily
with preparations.

Handling things till
we end the celebrations.

Worried then about
shortened days and
drifting long nights –

Afraid of ghosts and
lost in loving memories –

Climbing out of the rut,
yet dreaming of its end
and worried about calculations.

Ride the full moon,
peek at the snow and cold.

Unlock the door,
but keep it closed.
Check the yard.

Some late winter sun
will pull up the crocus –

And all life will begin.
The spring with rushing
colors crashing through –

Spirits awaken and
simple life begins.

Clear a path to the street.
Put out the birdseed.
Get to where you're going.

Then home again and
stay warm and cozy.

Travel the world
in your heart.
Keep the adventure simple.

Try not to slip.
Try not to fall.

Wait for a warm dawning
to a longer day
when the night doesn't close in.

It drifts by
and the stars blossom.

Mr. and Mrs. C. Came to Visit

On a chilly, windy day,
Mr. and Mrs. C. came to visit.
Never ones to stay,
they snacked and went their way.
As always, Mr. C. was over the top –
Type A personality, gaudy dresser
in and out, his day's work done.
Mrs. C. stands to the side,
a more conservative dresser
with those perfect color accents.
She's the more stable support
to Mr. C.'s flighty endeavors.
The others gathered around them
are just browns and grays,
drab and mundane in comparison
to their famous visitors.
Perhaps on to the next photo op
or off to find their spring home,
they are up, up and away,
a flash of bright red
followed by the accented missus.
Mr. and Mrs. Cardinal
leave the grackles, starlings and sparrows
to clean up their leftovers.

ON THE CELLAR DOOR

It is Over

It is over – The celebration, the preparation
and now we must wait for the signs.
The days are supposed to be longer,
but the rain makes them dull and restless.
When will the sun warm us again?
The wind has a bite that will not let go.
The ground must soften to part with
its colors and life.
The holiday decorations look out of place.
Our spirit is hung over, the children bored.
The nights are close, but too cold to be romantic –
It is drudgery till spring.
The first snow has dirtied, the snowman melted.
Ice becomes a hazard.
The ocean slips in and out
and seems lonesome and angry.
The trees shudder naked,
their covers hiding till warmth returns –
It is day after day
till flowers and life begin again.

The Naked Tree

It is December 26th. It is January 26th.
The tree stands naked and trembling.
A few short weeks ago, it stood proud –
The center of attention, the focal point,
limbs open and waiting to be festooned
with lights and decorations –
Causing some mild aggravation and then
children's screaming excitement.
Full-fledged, unabashed joy...
For the older folks, satisfaction,
and one late night, a tear
as an old hand brushes an ornament –
An old dangly thing hidden in the back
holding some unspoken memory.
The tree had witnessed the season
Christmas morning and the day following.
Now it is bare once more,
all the trimmings removed and put away.
Soon it will be crushed into a box
or dragged back outside
and cut up to be carted off
or spread around the yard.
The trail of needles leads to desolate winter,
the happy edge of that season now gone.
Those branches in the garden become curtains,
productive arms for the dirt dwellers
giving shelter to sleeping bulbs.
Together they lie close to each other
and the tree branches whisper secrets
to those that wait below –

Prisoner

I am a prisoner of the wind and rain,
of the gray, of my mind.
Only one third of winter gone
and the doors are heavy to open.
The outdoors almost doesn't exist.
Windows become picture frames,
for what is on the outside is not real.
Granted, the trees bend
and rain dots the canvas.
Perhaps silent televisions then,
with no remote to find a warmer channel.
The birds are silent actors,
darting to the feeders in moments of calm.
Remove my portable ears
and the silence is more intense.
I talk aloud to be sure of... What?
Of a normalcy? A comfort?
It is all self-inflicted.
I need only pick up the phone
and dial ten numbers, maybe eleven.
Then there will be voices –
Friends, strangers if I dialed wrong,
maybe my firstborn or the youngest,
perhaps only mechanical voices
because the originals have pushed open their doors
and so will I. It's not hard.
I'll shake the quiet from me
like a dog shakes the rain from head to toe.
It won't be long before windows open –
Maybe a fair day just fifty days from now.
Meanwhile, this old mutt will curl up by the fire
and chase my dreams with a little smile.

Winter Dance

Here they come from slate-colored sky –
Hundreds, thousands, no billions of dancers,
swirling and whirling around and around – round – round –
All dressed in white, no two alike.
Climbing, twisting, falling. Finally coming to rest.
Soundlessly crashing to the cold hard ground.
Piling next to and atop one another
till they wash away winter's weakening colors.

Quiet now watching the other dancers,
perhaps shifting in the wind's way,
finally resting, waiting for life.
Then a muffled grind. Twin spotlights
reach forward in the darkness.
Harshly the dance floor is cleared.
Thrown first to one side, then the other,
crushed and hardened, the music stops.

Now the hushed expectation of first light.
Sadly, come the janitors, pushing and lifting,
cleaning paths for their exit.
Grumbling about heavy and light,
throwing wide the space they need,
finally returning inside or huffing away for the day.

The sun has crawled tall,
and there's another burst from the door.
Bundled screams of delight fill the yellow light.
Now it's throwing and building and sliding.
"How's it packing?" Snowballs flying over snow forts,
hitting snowmen. "Oops! That's Mr. Griswald... Sorry."
Sleds, saucers and toboggans sliding down –
Some make the turn, others tumble out.
Rush to catch your breath and do it over again –
Over again till it's time to go in.

A day or two of this, then the dancers must leave.
Slowly slipping and running, melting into fallen rain.
All the same, once more coming up
and getting ready for the next invitation.
This year or next, this week or next –
Maybe later today.

Winter, Winter, Winter

I sit to see if my words have worth today –
With packages wrapped and set to deliver,
sadly the preparation is over.
A few days of pleasant exchanges –

But yesterday it began
and for most of three months
it will be here –
Winter, winter, winter.

I can't skate and don't want to –
I never could get a glide
after one, two...
and then my ankles turned in.

I can shovel, but I don't want to.
My fire burns electric.
My hot chocolate is instant.
It hasn't gotten cold, but…

I suppose I can still ride
a sled or a fiberglass saucer,
but I never belly-flopped –
I just sort of pushed off.

I've built snowmen and forts,
but I prefer "food-colored" monsters.
I know good packing snow –
That's the back-breaking snow.

Technically the days grow longer,
but with a worthless sun
it's small compensation
till the crocuses come.

Snowman

Oh... Oh, now I can see.
What a nice place to be!
Well, thank you.
Now it's easier to breath too.
What? Oh, neat!
I can talk to you.
I like your smile and laughter.
I'd like to give you a hug,
maybe that will come later.
Pretty! Pretty, but I don't need to be warm.
Ya know, I like just sitting here
and watching you
and being your friend –

Now don't worry about me.
I like watching you play,
building forts and having snowball fights,
and at night you go home,
get warm by the fire,
do your homework and have sweet dreams.
Me? I like looking at the stars
and watching the moon run across the sky.
In a few days, you may see me getting thinner,
but not to worry –
Even when I melt away
I'm in your heart every day.

There may come a time
when you're too big for snowmen,
but don't be upset.
We'll be hiding just out of sight
and when you see some kids
rolling the snow into balls,
just starting out,
we'll sneak up and push your lips into a smile.

A Winter Day

The bullies are at it.
First, the sun is so busy
putting a glare on the water
that it forgets to be warm.
Then, the wind
pushing the waves around,
wagging the wires
and dancing with the evergreens –
Everything but gentle.
An angry finch
sits on a branch by the window
loudly complaining about the day –
And I agree.
The sun has moved the clouds away.
The water's color has turned steel blue.
There is no invitation to be a part of this.
You're on your own, Bub.
Make it into something if you dare.
Don't just sit around and stare.
Look for moving rainbows,
listen for soft and comforting voices,
get into something worthwhile.
Feel your heart and sing,
even if off-key.
Dream and putter,
explore and stop staring.
Push your spirits up!

The bird has left,
gone to feed or hide,
tired of feathers pushed to down.
A tug pulls a barge
closer than usual.
I wonder if that struggle
is with the wind...
Ah! He's back, seeded up,
and still he continues the conversation.
Perhaps he's my closest neighbor –
A rhododendron resident.
But he pays no mortgage, no taxes.

Silly Winter

My toe doesn't want any more snow.
I'm in a rush to be rid of the slush.
Slippin' on ice is not nice –
Ya end up sittin' on your mittens.
I'm too old for the cold.
I'd rather go thud in the mud.
Romance is gone from the snowflake dance.
I want flora and fauna, maybe even a sauna.
I want to see faces and smiles, not thermostat dials.
I'm tired of snowmen and forts. I want fair weather reports –
Tell the frost to get lost!
Put your sled in the shed.
Christmas toys are movin' slow cause their batteries are low.
Get the gray to go away.
There's no reason to prolong the season.
I want green on the scene,
no sleet on my feet.
Let's exchange the ski for the tee!
How about the red of the rose instead of the nose?
I'm so depressed, I don't get dressed.
The sun is no fun.
And if my ears were my eyes and I cried,
then I'd have tears in my ears, my dears.

Winter Day

The sun warms through the window,
but snow and ice stand firm.
Kaleidoscoping clouds push eastward
sending some secret signal from heaven.
But I cannot translate it –
I do not understand.
It's all silly rabbits and spaceships.
The cylinder of sky rotates once more
as a bird cuts quickly to the west,
spotting a meal or joining friends.
Trees wiggle empty branches in the wind,
while evergreens bow to their partners
before the dance begins.
And so the day passes,
or minutes of the same,
a world outside a window –
Time with no name –
Standing apart and reaching out,
butting heads against the wall,
leaving fingerprints on the window.
Stepping out pulls your breath away.
Eyes must be narrowed
and the head tucked in.
The challenge of abandoning comfort,
boredom, monotony, routine and isolation
to search vainly for blossoms
and dreams hidden between steps.

Winter Relentless

The shivering night's depth
echoes winter's maddening pace.
This winter of storms
crawls with countless twenties and teens –
A rare touch of thirty-two
is then wind-chilled to single digits.
We fall in line and do our daily work.
What's to be done, is done,
but it is no fun –
This fuel to quell July's complaints
drags the New Year to Month Two,
with celebrations being filed with others past.
Two-thirds of the season still remains.
Happily we spent money on presents and decorations.
Now we must dig deeper
for gallons and cubic feet.
The walls of white narrow the roads
and cute little snowmen
are buried, toppled and forgotten.
All that love this are out of town.
They're on ridges and slopes and in chalets,
but there's something wrong –
They should have been made
to take all this along.

Winter Days...

Winter days have sharp edges.
The cold crisp air frames interiors.
Sunlight is just that, light.
It has no warmth, just illumination.
Evergreens host the only color.
Even houses beyond white and gray
offer only muted tones –
Perhaps a flash from the jogger or walker
sporting an outfit secured from a box
with a smile on Christmas morning.
Most of the birds are brown in motion.
Looking out from the cardigan sweater,
the bare branches seem to catch sight.
They call to the wind and it bends them –
Bends them toward you, waggles them,
maybe even has them slap the window...
Stay in! You're not wanted here.
The glass is a teasing barrier –
Just have to lift the window up.

Ha! Then winter can charge in,
and at least for a little while
sneer and chill your quaking bones.
Ultimately, you need food or company.
Your conversations with yourself
are empty and unrewarding.
You fill your pockets and bundle your body.
Swiftly, you exit your sanctuary.

Carefully, you negotiate the steps
watching for or dealing with
ice, snow, wind and the temperature.
You beeline for your mobile comfort zone,
but it is cold and angry.
"Now you want to start me up?"
Finally, its gizmos begin kicking in.
The sunshine is fatal on the horizon
and the temperature is falling,
falling through Fahrenheit
all the way to Celsius.
But the thing moves out.
You're on your way
at the worst part of the day.
What's left of the sun
shines below visors.
The magic of sunsets is weakened –
You are heading where? Out?
Where? Out of the house –
Away from the isolation.
Yet it follows you, it haunts you.
You seek shelter in a restaurant,
in a bar, in a store...
Small talk, noise, warmth,
different surroundings... Anything different.
There is jubilation in your heart
and still a caution somewhere
in the back of the mind.
At the end of the evening,
you still must drive home.

Snowflakes

Snowflakes softer than raindrops
gently wander down the sky,
caught by a lonesome wind,
twisting down in no special order,
touching down in an empty field
or on a little girl's waiting tongue.

Snowflakes driven sideways in a gale,
hurtling into the side of a fence
only to be swept up and relocated,
never settling through the night.
Finally the storm moves away.
Exhausted they rest waiting for shovel or plow.

Snowflakes crashing to earth,
full of moisture, just past sleet,
filling yards, covering automobiles,
waiting for the morning's sunshine –
Listening for the waddling architects
that will finally make them into men.

Another Winter Poem

It's that solitary time of winter
when tree branches bend
unnaturally to the ground,
like frosted fingers on a hag's hand
waiting for the Prince's kiss of spring
to make them beautiful again.

As the Snow Melts

As the snow melts,
the road is lined with frozen statuary,
hardy survivors in changing shapes,
prehistoric mud-covered monsters
slowly sinking into puddles –
Icebergs without an ocean.

As the snow melts,
it raises the curtain
on an interrupted spring.
The earliest flowers gather.
Each day their numbers increase,
while the ground softens to let them free.

As the snow melts,
tentative neighbors emerge,
chopping at a few remaining clusters
or just lingering outside,
relishing a newly felt freedom
from winter's voluntary hibernation.

As the snow melts,
our plans for the yard and garden
expand past any reasonable energy.
Everything is seen as lush green,
or bearing a large harvest
of fruit and color.

As the snow melts,
we see no crabgrass,
no dandelions or weeds.
No pests eat our crops.
No bugs or black and white friends
drive us back inside.

As the snow melts,
we are full of life
and projects that can be modified,
with new and renewed dreams
growing each day from
a budding, heart-filling optimism.

Moods of Winter

The many single moods of winter have begun.
No longer the grin of Christmas expectation.
New years begin alike with drunken celebration,
then the three-month recovery.

What is there in the winter
besides the first lasting snow?
Kittens near a radiator
and a love to share the long darkened hours.

There is the cold clear night
with the moon acting as
a blue streetlight to the world.
Water frozen still for blades of laughter.

Don't forget rosy little cheeks
and multicolored melting monsters,
hot chocolate and,
for some, a kindly fire.

What is there in the winter
for a lucky person like me?
There is a person to cuddle next to and dream,
to dream of the spring, summer, fall, winter.

To dream of the spring, summer, fall, winter –
Spring... Summer... Fall... And winter... A lifetime.

Good night.

DAVE GREGORY holds a BFA from Boston University's School of Fine and Applied Arts. (It's in the attic somewhere.)

He began writing in the 4th grade, though Miss Platt was never pleased with the quality of his penmanship.

He has written poetry and essays over the years, for his sanity and others' enjoyment. Published in several newspapers and poetry collections, he also had a poem published in a Christian publication that was distributed free in fourteen counties in Tennessee.

As for jobs, he has been, in no particular order, a light designer, built sets, acted, was a tour stage manager, assistant stage manager, production stage manager, and a newspaper boy. He has also been an Accounts Receivable clerk, Accounts Payable clerk, and office manager, flipped hamburgers, managed the Bernhard Center (Fine Arts Center) at the University of Bridgeport, managed a hardware store, worked in an electrical supply store, sold fertilizer, flowers, bushes, and Christmas trees (real and artificial), helped build mechanical indicators for airplanes and shutters for assorted uses, including one that is part of the Mars Rover.

Father of two and grandfather of three, Dave now reads to daycare children through the Literacy Center of Milford and is a docent, giving tours at the Milford Historical Society in Connecticut.